Bob—

YOU ARE

ONE

OF-A-KIND

Dave

P.S. Please ~~pray~~ that God
will use p. 265...

Published by SHIFTPOINTS, Inc.
www.SHIFTPOINTS.com

Version 4.0
Published September 2019
Copyright © 2019 David A. Ramos
All rights reserved.

The following are trademarks of SHIFTPOINTS Inc.:

- Drive One Direction®
- Decide One Thing. Align Everything. Win!®
- The Pit Stop Program®
- The Acceleration Index™
- The Navigation Index™
- Corporate Alignment Percentage™
- The SHIFTPOINTS logo

Company names, product names, and other brands referenced herein are the trademarks or registered trademarks of their respective owners.

ISBN 9781086196382

C⃝NTENTS

PART ONE – ALIGNMENT 101   **11**
SPEED READING – ALIGNMENT 101   13
ONE COMMON DENOMINATOR   15
ONE WORD   17
JOB ONE   19
ONE GENERATION   21
ONE SCALE   23
ONE ROOT CAUSE   25
ONE QUESTION   27
ONE FORMULA   29
ONE-OF-A-KIND   31
ONE AND ONLY ONE   33
ONE TEAM – WHAT DOES TEAM MEAN?   35
ONE DIRECTION   37
SUMMARY – ALIGNMENT 101   39

PART TWO – THE ACCELERATORS   **41**
THE TWELVE ACCELERATORS   43

ONE TEAM   **45**
SPEED READING – ONE TEAM   47
FORD   49
THE CARLYLE GROUP   51
BERKSHIRE HATHAWAY   53
VALIANT   55
SUMMARY – ONE TEAM   57

ONE THING   **59**
SPEED READING – ONE THING   61
DYSON   63
HERMAN MILLER   65
FERRARI   67
BTI360   69
SUMMARY – ONE THING   71

ONE VISION   73

SPEED READING – ONE VISION   75
VIRGIN HYPERLOOP ONE   77
HABITAT FOR HUMANITY   79
SOUTHWEST AIRLINES   81
MOTHERS AGAINST DRUNK DRIVING   83
SUMMARY – ONE VISION   85

ONE MISSION   87

SPEED READING – ONE MISSION   89
AMAZON   91
TESLA   93
MEDTRONIC   95
ONE.ORG   97
SUMMARY – ONE MISSION   99

ONE CODE   101

SPEED READING – ONE CODE   103
BLOMMER CHOCOLATE   105
HILTON HOTELS   107
MAYO CLINIC   109
NETFLIX   111
SUMMARY – ONE CODE   113

ONE BRAND   115

SPEED READING – ONE BRAND   117
VIRGIN   119
UPS   121
GOVERNMENT EMPLOYEES INSURANCE COMPANY   123
CHICK-FIL-A   125
DE BEERS   127
SUMMARY – ONE BRAND   129

ONE STRATEGY   131

SPEED READING – ONE STRATEGY   133
USAA   135
BASECAMP   137
IRIDIUM   139
DOLLAR TREE   141
TOMS   143
SUMMARY – ONE STRATEGY   145

ONE PORTFOLIO | **147**
SPEED READING – ONE PORTFOLIO | 149
BMW | 151
LEGO | 153
RYOBI | 155
HUBSPOT | 157
SUMMARY – ONE PORTFOLIO | 159

ONE WAY | **161**
SPEED READING – ONE WAY | 163
BOGNET CONSTRUCTION | 165
FORMULA ONE | 167
STARBUCKS | 169
ING | 171
SUMMARY – ONE WAY | 173

ONE WOW! | **175**
SPEED READING – ONE WOW! | 177
RITZ-CARLTON | 179
COSTCO | 181
CROSSFIT® | 183
FOUR SISTERS | 185
SUMMARY – ONE WOW! | 187

ONE PLAN | **189**
SPEED READING – ONE PLAN | 191
GOOGLE | 193
SALESFORCE | 195
IDEXX | 197
HAGERTY | 199
SUMMARY – ONE PLAN | 201

EVERYONE | **203**
SPEED READING – EVERYONE | 205
23ANDME | 207
CIRQUE DU SOLEIL | 209
MCKINSEY AND COMPANY | 211
PUBLIX | 213
SIMPLEXITY | 215
AMERICAN RED CROSS | 217
SUMMARY – EVERYONE | 219

SUMMARY – THE ACCELERATORS   **221**
   SUMMARY – THE ACCELERATORS   222
   SELECT ONE BIG ONE   224

PART THREE – DRIVE ONE DIRECTION   **227**
   SPEED READING – DRIVE ONE DIRECTION   229
   MAKE ALIGNMENT JOB ONE   231
   RUN A ONE-COMPANY CAMPAIGN   233
   BUILD A ONE-COMPANY CULTURE   235
   DEVELOP ONE SYSTEM   237
   LEVERAGE ONE MODEL   239
   DELIVER ONE MESSAGE   241
   APPLY ONE PROCESS   243
   WORK AS ONE   245
   UTILIZE ONE STYLE   247
   MEET ONE-ON-ONE   249
   PLAN ON ONE DECADE   251
   START WITH ONE PERSON   253
   SUMMARY – DRIVE ONE DIRECTION   255

PART FOUR – MORE RESOURCES   **257**
   ONE FORD – THE EXPECTED BEHAVIORS   259
   ONE LIFE STAGE   261
   ONE OPERATING MODEL   263
   ONE BOOK   265
   ONE PLATFORM   267
   ONE SONG – "KUMBAYA"   269

SOURCES AND REFERENCES   **271**

ABOUT SHIFTPOINTS   **272**

ABOUT DAVE RAMOS   **273**

FOREWRD

By Alan R. Mulally

I spent thirty-seven years at Boeing, eight years at Ford, and have been a Director at Alphabet since 2014. These experiences convinced me of one thing:

Alignment is the ultimate competitive advantage.

At Boeing, alignment is a key part of the corporate culture. In fact, "Operate as One Boeing" is one of three components of their strategy.

When I became the President and CEO of the Ford Motor Company in 2006, I knew that improving alignment was critical to our survival and long-term success. That is why we implemented the ONE FORD plan.

This started with getting all of our stakeholders— employees, dealers, investors, suppliers, and our union—to operate as One Team. A key component of building this culture of teamwork was the "Sixteen Expected Behaviors." (These are listed in the More Resources section for your review.)

The second component was One Plan. This involved aggressively restructuring the company, accelerating product development, and improving our balance sheet.

Third, we aligned everyone with One Goal, "An exciting and viable Ford that delivered Profitable Growth for All (PGA)."

Finally, we used a robust management system that included Business Plan Reviews every Thursday to keep everyone aligned. You can learn more about the ONE FORD plan in the case study.

Serving on the Alphabet Board of Directors has been a fascinating experience. Alphabet creates alignment in many ways, most notably with the Objectives and Key Results (OKR) methodology. You can learn more about OKRs in the Google case study, and in my friend John Doerr's excellent book, *Measure What Matters*.

In summary, every company, regardless of size, must create alignment. *Drive One Direction* provides a comprehensive guide for any leader who wants to unleash the accelerating power of alignment for their company. The book features a wide variety of fascinating case studies, combined with practical guidelines for how to apply these best practices in your company.

I hope you enjoy reading it as much as I have!!!

Alan

THANK YOU

First, thank you for reading my book.

I hope you enjoy reading it as much as I enjoyed writing it.

Next, a huge thank you to my wife, Twee. She has been the greatest partner a guy could ever ask for. She is my One and Only.

Thanks to my beta testers who read Version One. You confirmed my core hypothesis and encouraged me to invest One More Year to make the book even better.

A special thank you to Larry Hitchcock, my Harvard Business School classmate who is a partner at Deloitte. His very thorough and specific feedback inspired me to create the ***Drive One Direction***® methodology.

In early 2018, I printed preview editions of the book. Dozens of people, including my dad, my brothers, Ken Blackwell, Kim Croyle, Shamik Daru, Paul Gault, Bob Gregory, Lee Harper, Paul Hayre, Jillian Hufnagel, Bob Korzeniewski, Jerry McMahan, Jeff Minsky, Lou Morsberger, Tyler Paris, Tara Rethore, Adam Schmidt, Sherri Sklar, and Steve Smith provided exceptionally helpful feedback, suggestions, and corrections.

As part of my research, I had the privilege of personally interviewing One Hundred CEOs.

Every CEO contributed to this book. However, I would like to start by extending a special thank-you to Alan Mulally, the retired CEO of Ford. In many ways, his ONE FORD plan shaped my thinking about the importance of alignment. In fact, during my interview, he affirmed my core hypothesis: alignment is the ultimate competitive advantage.

He went on to express his enthusiasm for my book and even stated that he thought it would become a bestseller!

In addition to Alan, I would like to extend my sincerest thanks to Randy Papadellis, the retired CEO of Ocean Spray. Although I have been using the term "Chief Alignment Officer" for many years, he is the first CEO that I discovered who actually used that term to describe himself.

A heartfelt shout-out to Chris Whytal. Chris is the incredible graphic designer who created the SHIFTPOINTS visual identity, the cover design, the ONE icons, and all of the other graphics. He helped bring the book—and the SHIFTPOINTS brand—to life.

Thanks to Sarah Madden, who graciously edited my manuscripts. She became the grammar teacher I never had.

Thanks to Jennifer Whittenberg. She was SHIFTPOINTS employee Number One. I'm grateful for your continued support, encouragement, and friendship.

Thanks to Bain and Company. They were my go-to source for research and validation and I am grateful that they share their wisdom in a way that mere mortals can understand.

Finally, thank God I finally finished this book. Seriously, I must thank God for sustaining me through this process.

Writing this book was the hardest thing I have ever done.

PART ONE

ALIGNMENT 101

"Alignment is the ultimate competitive advantage!"

Dave Ramos
Founder and CEO
SHIFTPOINTS, Inc.

SPEED READING – ALIGNMENT 101

The United States Military has an acronym called BLUF, which stands for Bottom Line Up Front.

Here is my BLUF: Alignment is the ultimate competitive advantage.

I came to that conclusion after studying over three hundred companies of all shapes, sizes, and industries.

In addition, as part of my research, I interviewed over One Hundred CEOs.

Finally, we read "every book ever written" about alignment and dozens of white papers and scholarly articles.

We distilled our findings into The Twelve Foundational Principles of Alignment. They are:

1. Misalignment is an extremely common, pervasive problem that plagues organizations of all types.

2. There is no standard definition for alignment … so we developed One.

3. Alignment is mission-critical for *every* organization. That is why we say, "Alignment is Job One."

4. Alignment is infinitely more complicated and difficult than it was just One Generation ago.

5. The complexity of alignment increases exponentially as the company grows, driven by three factors: the number of employees, the number of divisions, and the number of locations.

6. Misalignment is the root cause of virtually every organizational—and interpersonal—dysfunction.

7. There is no generally accepted metric to measure alignment ... so we developed the One-Question "Corporate Alignment Percentage™ (CAP)" assessment.

8. Misalignment is extremely costly ... and improving alignment might be the highest ROI activity any organization can undertake.

9. Each company must create alignment in a unique One-of-a-Kind Way. This is driven by your life stage, operating model, and business philosophy.

10. Alignment is primarily created at the corporate level. This utilizes the "One and Only One" model.

11. Teamwork is the foundation of alignment, but you must answer the question, "What does team mean?"

12. Highly aligned companies dramatically outperform their fragmented competitors. That is why we call them "fast-lane companies."

We think of The Twelve Principles as "Alignment 101." In the following pages, we will be expanding on each of them.

As you will notice, I use the word "One" a lot. (My wife says I have a One-Track Mind. Of course, if she says it, it must be true!)

Actually, I use the word "One" over and over because it is the best word to describe alignment. It is also the word that virtually every CEO we interviewed used.

Some may find this trite or kitschy. Some—especially the grammarians and purists—might find it irritating that I always capitalize it.

Nonetheless, I hope you find the ideas in the book to be One(s) worth considering.

ONE COMMON DENOMINATOR

In 1995, I was promoted to VP of Marketing Communications for a division of Nortel Networks.

It was my first exposure to the devastating impact of misalignment.

I discovered that my division had thirty-seven different advertising, branding, and public relations agencies. And our materials made us look like we were thirty-seven different companies. There were different sizes. Different color schemes. Different designs. Different taglines.

Theoretically, Nortel was selling a portfolio of networking equipment designed to help customers build a seamless network. I remember asking my team, "How can we expect customers to believe we can build a seamless network when we can't even get our brochures to fit in the same folder?"

Over the next three years, we aligned everything. We went from thirty-seven agencies to two. We developed a unifying theme and a consistent value proposition.

Our team won The Chairman's Award, Nortel's highest honor, for our work.

Shortly thereafter, Nortel acquired Bay Networks in a $7.1B transaction, one of the largest networking deals of that time. I was promoted to Vice President of Global Marketing for the new Nortel/Bay division and we moved to San Jose, California.

Mergers are always challenging, but this was a colossal mess. In this case, it was not just the marketing collateral that was out of alignment. Everything was out of alignment.

We had two CEOs. Two cultures. Two agendas. Two visions. Two of everything.

To integrate the global marketing team, I launched an initiative called One Team. We had our first global marketing conference. There was a glimmer of hope.

One month later, my boss—who was from Bay Networks—called me into his office and fired me. Less than One Year after winning the Chairman's Award, I was gone.

We moved back to Washington, D.C., and I joined a software startup called AnswerLogic. The vision was to develop a natural language search engine. We called it an answer engine, and the concept was brilliant.

Unfortunately, the founder and the president could not agree on which market to target, what product to build, or how to build it. They fought constantly. To make matters worse, the board could not agree either. The company failed, and $11M in venture capital went down the drain.

All caused by a lack of alignment.

After a year or so, I did a consulting project for the Pentagon. Their problem? Lack of alignment.

Then, I started doing some pro-bono consulting for our church, McLean Bible Church, a mega-church in Virginia with 15,000 attendees. The church was the most fragmented organization I had ever encountered. Every ministry was a complete silo.

Five radically different and tragically dysfunctional organizations. One Common Denominator: massive dysfunction caused by a lack of alignment.

Now you know why I felt compelled to write this book.

ONE WORD

Alignment. [A·**line**·ment]. One word. Three syllables. Thousands of applications.

But, what does alignment actually mean?

The etymology of "align" is French. Webster's says the first known use of the word was in 1693. Some of the common uses include:

- to arrange things or people in a straight line.

- to bring things or people into alignment.

- to bring people into agreement with a particular group, party, cause, etc.

- to bring things into a proper coordination (such as the wheels of a car).

Align is a verb. *Aligned* is a past participle. *Aligning* is a gerund. *Alignment* is a noun.

Okay, enough of that. What does alignment mean for your company?

There are three dimensions of corporate alignment:

First, companies must be *externally* aligned. That means that their vision, strategies, goals, etc. must be aligned with market realities and customer expectations. Since the external environment is constantly changing, companies must be both aligned and agile.

In fact, the ability to quickly realign the entire company to meet changing external conditions is mission-critical. We call this "aligned agility." Companies who create this capability have a tremendous competitive advantage.

Second, using the standard organization chart as an illustration, companies must be *vertically* aligned. On the vertical dimension, the corporate headquarters team develops visions, values, strategies, goals, priorities, plans, policies, and more. Every division, department, team, and individual must align with the things that come "down" from corporate.

Finally, again, using the organization chart as an illustration, companies must be *horizontally* aligned. That means that divisions must align with each other. Europe must align with Asia. Marketing must align with sales.

The Hatfields must align with the McCoys.

In summary, here is my working definition of alignment: an optimal state where everyone—and everything—is externally aligned with market realities, vertically aligned with corporate priorities, and horizontally aligned to leverage the full resources of the company to win.

In my working definition, I use the term "everyone and everything." Companies have both people and things.

Aligning *things* means that there is only One Version. For example, you must eliminate conflicting versions of key documents. (One client inadvertently had multiple old versions of their mission, vision, and values circulating around. Those multiple versions created confusion.)

Aligning things also means that those things deliver One Message. In other words, your vision statements, mission statements, strategies, policies, goals, products, metrics, systems, etc. must be in alignment with each other.

Aligning *people* means you must align them with your things, *and* you must align them with each other.

I hope you like my definition. If not, perhaps you should gather your team and write your own.

JOB ONE

We believe that every organization, regardless of size or industry or operating model, must create strategic alignment.

That is why we say, "Alignment is Job One."

For every idea, there are contrarians. Alignment is no exception.

So, let's consider the question: is alignment really necessary for every organization?

Consider some of the common objections to alignment raised by my contrarian friends:

- Can't you just let everyone do whatever they feel is right?

- Won't top-down controls stifle innovation and creativity?

- Do you really need rules?

- Won't people just naturally self-align to do what is in the corporation's best interest?

- What, are we going to all join hands and sing "Kumbaya"? (see the More Resources section for the words!)

After all, you can't legislate morality.

Perhaps you are an alignment contrarian. Perhaps you have these questions and more. If so, consider these examples:

In 2014, the online retailer Zappos adopted a utopian "self-management" model called Holacracy. When Zappos adopted it, hundreds of managerial positions were eliminated. It was hailed as the future of work. Fully empowered employees. Free to contribute. Free to innovate. Free from creativity-stifling management.

Not so much. The Holacracy model has a formal constitution that is 42 pages long.

Consider Burning Man, the annual festival in the Nevada desert. It is designed to be the ultimate, utopian experience of individual freedom and "radical self-expression." It attracts over 70,000 people from all walks of life (including, ironically, billionaires who fly in on private jets).

But even Burning Man has rules to keep everyone aligned.

Yes, but how about the anarchists?

The International Anarchist Federation is fighting for "the abolition of all forms of authority whether economical, political, social, religious, cultural or sexual." Interestingly, to become a member, you must agree to align with their statement of principles.

Amazing. Even anarchists need alignment.

I hope these examples help convince you that alignment is mission-critical for every organization.

ONE GENERATION

My dad went to work at General Electric in January 1962.

In just One Generation, the workforce has radically changed, and creating alignment is now radically more difficult.

In my dad's generation, the workforce was very homogeneous. Most of the "white collar" workers were white males. Most of the women in the workforce were in secretarial roles.

Now, the workforce is tremendously and beautifully diverse. The increase in diversity is a great thing. Let me say that again; the increase in diversity is a great thing, but it does make alignment much more difficult.

In my dad's generation, a large percentage of the workforce had military experience. They were comfortable in top-down, command-and-control organizations. They were trained to obey orders.

Now, the workforce is radically different. Many were raised in the "me" generation. Millennials have a very different worldview. As a result, the old command-and-control way of creating alignment is no longer effective.

In my dad's generation, there was a basic civility and decency in society. Children were trained to say, "Yes, Ma'am" or "Yes, Sir." Politicians referred to each other as "distinguished colleagues." There was a respect for authority.

Now, people denigrate each other every night on TV. They attack each other in social media. They shoot the police. This makes alignment much more difficult.

In my dad's generation, many companies had either explicit or implicit guarantees of lifetime employment. My dad spent thirty-one years with GE. When I started at IBM in 1979, the company still had a culture of lifetime employment.

Now, the workforce is extremely unsettled, and most people will work for multiple companies in their careers. Companies expect loyalty, but they don't give it in return. This makes alignment much more difficult.

In my dad's generation, the majority of people working at a company were officially classified as employees.

Now, the workforce is an ever-changing mix of employees, long-term contractors, temporaries, and gig workers. This creates multiple classes of workers with different benefits, different rules, different loyalties, and different goals. This makes alignment much more difficult.

In my dad's generation, when you wanted to communicate with someone who worked in your building, you walked down the hall.

Now, people send an email to the person sitting in the next cubicle. This makes alignment much more difficult.

In my dad's generation, companies had physical offices.

Now, many companies have large numbers of full- and part-time telecommuters. Some companies, such as Zapier, are 100 percent virtual.

In my dad's generation, the Fortune 500 was extremely stable: companies remained on the list for an average of sixty-one years.

Now, the average tenure of a Fortune 500 company is fifteen years. Companies that were models of stability—like Arthur Andersen, Nortel Networks, and Lehman Brothers—are completely gone.

The combination of these organizational and societal forces has made alignment radically more difficult.

ONE SCALE

When companies are small, they are in One Business. They target One Market. They sell One Product. There is One P&L. Everyone probably sits in One Office.

But, as companies grow, the complexity of creating alignment scales exponentially.

Just to be clear, even small, One Business businesses can have alignment problems. (We've even worked with solopreneurs, otherwise known as One Person Companies, who had alignment problems.)

But the larger you are, the more likely you will struggle with alignment.

The complexity of aligning an organization is driven by three factors: the number of divisions, the number of locations, and the number of countries.

As companies grow, they create divisions. There is only One Problem: divisions—by definition—divide.

When companies create divisions, they must align the divisions with corporate *and* they must align the divisions with each other.

In addition, each division adds its own strategies, goals, standards, priorities, policies, etc. to the things that cascaded down from corporate. Then, departments are expected to align with both the things that cascaded down from corporate *and* the things that cascaded down from the divisions.

In addition, as companies grow, they expand geographically. Most companies follow a predictable pattern. They expand from local to regional to national to multinational and ultimately become truly global companies.

However, the broader your geographic footprint, the harder it is to create alignment.

Even opening a second office in the same city can cause misalignment problems. We recently learned of a company that had one office in downtown Washington, D.C., and another office in Tysons Corner, Virginia. They were only fifteen miles apart, but the company had become badly fragmented, and the two offices fought constantly. The CEO ultimately decided to shut both offices down and move to a new, neutral location.

Finally, expanding globally sounds like a great strategy, but companies must consider the implications for alignment.

Multiple languages, multiple currencies. More travel. More complexity.

McKinsey calls this the "globalization penalty," and their research showed that global companies consistently scored lower than locally focused companies on several dimensions of organizational health.

In summary, the alignment challenge grows *exponentially* as your company grows. To quantify this, SHIFTPOINTS developed the Alignment Complexity Index™ (ACI).

To calculate your Alignment Complexity Index™ (ACI), multiple your #Divisions x #Locations x #Countries.

Alignment is a universal challenge. The more divisions, locations, and countries you have, the harder it becomes.

ONE ROOT CAUSE

I believe that the root cause of virtually every organizational problem is misalignment.

Why do I believe that? Let me count the ways!

When your market vision is misaligned, you miss growth opportunities.

When your business model is misaligned, you lose money.

When your human resources strategy is misaligned, you hire the wrong people.

When your product development team is misaligned, you build the wrong product.

When your operating model is misaligned, people spend endless hours in internal coordination meetings.

When your mission-critical processes are misaligned, you miss your deadlines and irritate your customers.

When your management system is misaligned, decisions are frequently overturned.

When marketing and sales are misaligned, you miss your revenue targets.

When management and labor are misaligned, workers go on strike.

When the board and the CEO are misaligned, the CEO gets fired.

I could go on, but you get the point: *misalignment is the root cause of virtually every organizational dysfunction.*

We also see misalignment as the root cause of most interpersonal conflicts.

For example, recently I was coaching an executive who was struggling to meet his numbers. I asked him, "Why are you missing your numbers?"

He gave me an explanation that seemed plausible, but then I asked, "Would your boss agree with that explanation?"

"Probably not."

Given that the executive and his boss were not aligned on the root cause of the problem, there was little chance that they would agree on the executive's proposed solution.

In another session, a different executive was recounting her accomplishments. Again, I asked the question, "Would your boss agree with that list?"

"Probably not."

In both cases, the executives and their bosses were misaligned.

Alignment is both a strategic corporate issue and a tactical interpersonal one.

That is why improving alignment is Job One!

ONE QUESTION

A few months ago, I went to the car dealer for maintenance. As I entered the service bay, I drove over a special sensor on the ground that measured my alignment in real-time.

I was dismayed to learn that my car was out of alignment.

That's right, the guy who was writing a book about alignment called *Drive One Direction* was driving a car that was out of alignment.

Imagine my shame!

I did some research and discovered that the system was made by Hunter Engineering Company in Bridgeton, Missouri (www.hunter.com). Here is what I learned:

"Hunter's patented alignment check system is the quickest way to measure alignment angles that affect tire life. The test takes less than a minute to produce total toe and camber measurements for both axles. Results are displayed in easy-to-understand, color-coded graphics."

Ever since that experience, I wanted to create a radically simple way for companies to measure their alignment.

During my CEO interviews, I always asked them about the importance of alignment.

"Alignment is mission-critical," was the Number One answer.

Then, I would ask them about the old adage, "If you can't measure it, you can't manage it."

Every CEO gave me the same answer, "I totally agree with that!"

Then, I would go on to say, "So, you told me that alignment was mission-critical … and if you can't measure something you can't manage it."

"That's right!"

"So, how do you measure alignment?"

At this point, there would be a long and awkward pause …

Measuring alignment is a complicated problem. However, to get things started, we developed a simple One Question survey:

> On a scale of 1 to 100, rate your company's current level of strategic alignment.
>
> 1 = We are like a group of warring tribes. Civil war about to break out.
>
> 100 = We are like a perfectly synchronized rowing crew.

Go ahead … answer the question for your company … what's your number? We call this your Corporate Alignment Percentage™ (CAP).

Perhaps you are drawn to the simplicity of the CAP model. Perhaps you feel the need for a more "sophisticated" approach. Regardless, we believe it is essential for your company to develop a way to measure alignment. There are three primary reasons.

First, strategic alignment is mission-critical. You simply cannot succeed without it. Second, strategic alignment is a leading indicator. Third, strategic alignment is EveryOne's business. Thus, EveryOne can improve the metric.

So, how does your company measure alignment?

ONE FORMULA

The classic illustration of alignment is the rowing crew.

But imagine an eight-person boat with only seven rowers.

Or worse yet, imagine that one of the rowers is rowing in the opposite direction.

Misaligned crews lose the race. Misaligned companies lose millions.

But how much does misalignment cost your company?

Fortunately, you can calculate the cost of misalignment.

Let's say your company has 1,000 employees, and your Corporate Alignment Percentage is 80 percent.

That means that 20 percent of your employees' time and energy is wasted … which is the equivalent of 200 people lost.

You are paying for 1,000 people, but only getting the energy of 800. If your average loaded cost per person is $100,000 per year, that is the equivalent of 20 million dollars!

Now, you should do your own math.

What is your total payroll? What is your Corporate Alignment Percentage?

How much is misalignment costing your company? Conversely, how much value can your company recapture by improving alignment?

Perhaps an illustration will help you understand the benefits of improving alignment.

A few years ago, I owned a twin turbocharged BMW.

In case you don't have a degree in automotive engineering, let me explain how a turbocharger works.

In a normal engine, gasoline is mixed with air and is then ignited by the spark plug to produce power. This process is not 100 percent efficient, so hot gases flow out the exhaust pipes into the environment.

A turbocharger is a small device that looks like a fan. It "recycles" the hot exhaust gases and forces them back into the engine. It converts the energy that would otherwise have been wasted into additional horsepower.

Alignment is the turbocharger of organizational performance.

The **Drive One Direction®** process "recycles" the energy that is wasted by misalignment and turns it into additional people power.

This enables you to zoom past your competition!

My assertion is that improving alignment is likely the highest ROI activity you have.

ONE-OF-A-KIND

I strongly believe that alignment is Job One.

But every company must create alignment in a unique, One-of-a-Kind Way.

Three primary factors impact your company's approach to creating alignment.

The first factor is your company's life stage. Startups are worried about survival, and spinouts are focused on cutting the corporate umbilical cord. (See the One Life Stage chapter in the More Resources section for more details.)

The second factor is your company's operating model. (See the One Operating Model chapter in the More Resources section for more details.) Some companies run like denominations, and some churches run like corporations.

The third factor is your company's business philosophy.

When you combine these three factors, the result is thousands of unique permutations.

However, regardless of your company's unique situation, alignment is mission-critical.

Our goal was to develop One Methodology that would work for every company, regardless of life stage, operating model, or business philosophy.

This led us to develop the **Drive One Direction®** methodology.

We believe that every company, regardless of life stage, operating model, or business philosophy, can—and should— apply the **Drive One Direction®** methodology. However, every company should do so in a unique, One-of-a-Kind Way.

For example, every company has a corporate brand. Your job is to create a unique, One-of-a-Kind Brand.

Every company has a corporate culture. You must create a unique, One-of-a-Kind Culture.

Developing a One-of-a-Kind Way of creating alignment will differentiate you from your competitors. It will allow you to create a unique One-of-a-Kind Company.

Some of the exemplar companies, such as Amazon, use the term "DNA" to articulate their unique approach to creating alignment. We like that, since your DNA both identifies who you are and differentiates you from everyone else.

Alignment is Job One, but every company must create it in a unique, One-of-a-Kind Way.

ONE AND ONLY ONE

Corporate. [**core**-per-it]. Adjective – pertaining to a united group.

A key insight from the exemplar companies is that they created alignment at the corporate level.

The strongest form of alignment is the "One and Only One" model. You literally have One and Only One for the entire company.

No divisions, departments, geographies, or functions can have a different one. Your One and Only One(s) are absolutely, positively, and nonnegotiably the same everywhere in your company.

For example, Tesla has One—and Only One—Mission Statement. Netflix has One—and Only One—Code of Conduct. Bognet has One—and Only One—Way.

In most cases, these items are *exactly* the same everywhere. In some cases, they are *essentially* the same. (For example, your One Tagline might be translated into other languages.)

You might think this is obvious, but many organizations will handle this differently.

For example, you might think every company should have One—and Only One—Mission Statement. But we have worked with companies where every division, department, and team had its own mission statement, none of which was linked in any way to the corporate mission statement.

But surely, every company has One List of core values. Nope. (As you will discover in the Hilton case study, at one time they had thirty different lists!)

Making something a One—and Only One—Corporate Standard is simple to understand, highly effective, very efficient, and very easy to enforce.

Of course, it can also be perceived as too centralized and too controlling. Sometimes, One Size does not fit all.

One Vision might not fit all business units. One Expense Policy might not be fair to all locations. The fashionistas might rebel against having One Dress Code.

Some companies create alignment with many Corporate One and Only One(s). Others delegate more autonomy to their divisions or operating companies.

The corporate executive team should carefully balance the need for centralized control with the desire to empower EveryOne.

So, your company must decide.

What must be absolutely, positively, and nonnegotiably the same everywhere?

ONE TEAM – WHAT DOES TEAM MEAN?

A lot has been written about teamwork.

Teamwork is the foundation of alignment.

But many people have never been on a high-performance team, thus they do not have a real framework or experience base to work from. They don't really know what "team" means.

In addition, there are many kinds of teams:

A crew team is a homogeneous group. Each member has a virtually identical build and an identical skill-set. There is only One Team, and they must work in perfect harmony in order to win. They are all—quite literally—in the same boat!

A golf team is a loose collection of individuals, all playing their own games. The team wins if enough people win their individual matches. However, it is possible for an individual player to win the individual trophy, yet have their team lose the match.

An improvisational jazz band is a different kind of team altogether. There is no conductor, no playbook, no scoreboard, no trophy, no match to win or lose, and no coxswain to keep everyone synchronized. Yet, the musicians demonstrate amazing teamwork.

A football team is a highly interdependent group of diverse players. Each player has very specialized skills. While there are sub-teams—offense, defense, and special teams—there is only one winner at end of the game. They win or lose as a team.

In 2015, retired General Stanley McChrystal discussed the complexity of sub-teams in his book, *Team of Teams*. In many companies, the real issue is that people are aligned with their "sub-team" but are not aligned with the other teams or with corporate.

- The Boston office is tight, but they don't get along with the New York office.

- The marketing team is tight, but they don't get along with sales.

- The corporate finance team is tight, but they don't get along with the divisions.

- The European team is tight, but they don't get along with the Americans.

- The Democrats are tight, but they don't get along with the Republicans.

People tend to get along with their immediate group. Their function. Their local office. Their clan. Their tribe. But they fight with people who are not part of their group.

So, as you embark on the journey to improve alignment, perhaps you should start by answering One Simple Question, "What does 'team' mean?"

ONE DIRECTION

Imagine a fleet of vehicles.

All of them driving in One Direction, dynamically aligned with a navigation system that can reroute the fleet on a dime.

That was the vision that inspired this book and led us to trademark the term **Drive One Direction**®.

Over ten years ago, I started a consulting firm to help companies improve alignment. In fact, my original code name for the business was "aligned.org." While I did not use that as our company name, alignment has been our focus since the beginning.

Over the past decade, we have worked with dozens of companies. We studied hundreds of organizations of all shapes, sizes, and industries. And, as I mentioned, I interviewed One Hundred CEOs.

All of this led me to develop the twelfth foundational principle: highly aligned companies dramatically outperform their fragmented competitors.

Specifically, highly aligned companies excel in three areas:

- **Revenue Growth:** Exemplar companies such as Salesforce, Basecamp, and Hagerty grew at incredible rates, and their CEOs specifically attributed their revenue growth to their high level of alignment.

- **Employee Engagement:** Highly aligned companies, such as BTI360, Publix, and McKinsey, are perennial Best Places to Work award winners.

- **Customer Engagement:** Exemplar companies, such as Southwest, Mayo Clinic, and USAA leveraged high levels of alignment to ensure that they deliver on their brand promise. These companies have industry-leading NetPromoter® scores.

Many of the exemplar companies we identified, such as The Carlyle Group, Salesforce, and Amazon committed to alignment from Day One. Driven by prior experience working for fragmented companies, their founders had the wisdom to build their new companies on a foundation of alignment.

Obviously, this is the best-case scenario.

However, many companies, including Ford, Microsoft, and Starbucks, successfully implemented "One Company" campaigns to realign organizations that had become highly fragmented. In all three cases, the stock price more than doubled in the years following the launch of the alignment initiative.

Thus, it is possible to realign a highly fragmented company.

In summary, our research led us to conclude that highly aligned companies dramatically outperform their misaligned competitors.

That is why we call them "fast-lane companies."

SUMMARY – ALIGNMENT 101

I opened this chapter with a BLUF.

Alignment is the ultimate competitive advantage.

Many companies will *say* they agree with that idea. But the exemplar companies are passionately and unwaveringly committed to it.

In **Part One – *Alignment 101***, we covered The Twelve Foundational Principles of Alignment. To summarize:

1. Misalignment is an extremely common, pervasive problem that plagues organizations of all types.

2. There is no standard definition for alignment … so we developed One.

3. Alignment is mission-critical for *every* organization. That is why we say, "Alignment is Job One."

4. Alignment is infinitely more complicated and difficult than it was just One Generation ago.

5. The complexity of alignment increases exponentially as the company grows.

6. Misalignment is the root cause of virtually every organizational—and interpersonal—dysfunction.

7. There is no generally accepted metric to measure alignment … so we developed the One-Question "Corporate Alignment Percentage™ (CAP)" assessment.

8. Misalignment is extremely costly … and improving alignment might be the highest ROI activity any organization can undertake.

9. Each company must create alignment in a unique One-of-a-Kind Way.

10. Alignment is primarily created at the corporate level. This utilizes the "One and Only One" model.

11. Teamwork is the foundation of alignment, but you must answer the question, "What does team mean?"

12. Highly aligned companies dramatically outperform their fragmented competitors. That is why we call them "fast-lane companies."

Alignment creates speed. That is why we call it the accelerating power of alignment.

So, how do companies unleash the accelerating power of alignment? The rest of the book will answer that question.

Our goal is to have your company Driving in One Direction.

PART TWO

THE
ACCELERATORS

THE ACCELERATORS

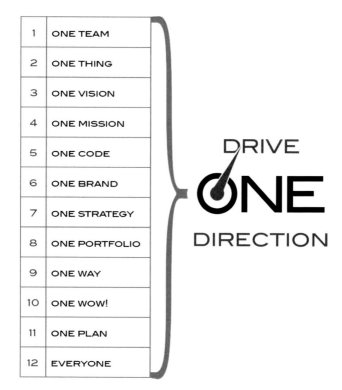

1	ONE TEAM
2	ONE THING
3	ONE VISION
4	ONE MISSION
5	ONE CODE
6	ONE BRAND
7	ONE STRATEGY
8	ONE PORTFOLIO
9	ONE WAY
10	ONE WOW!
11	ONE PLAN
12	EVERYONE

DRIVE

ONE

DIRECTION

ALIGNMENT IS THE ULTIMATE COMPETITIVE ADVANTAGE

THE TWELVE ACCELERATORS

Alignment is a complex, multidimensional problem.

Therefore, aligning your company requires an integrated, multidisciplinary approach.

The **Drive One Direction**® methodology includes twelve components. We call these components "The Twelve Accelerators." As you will see, each has the word "One."

One Team. One Vision. One Strategy.

The next section of the book has twelve short chapters.

Each chapter begins with a short introduction called a "Speed Reading." Each Speed Reading is just One Page long.

Next, we examine companies that exemplified that way of creating alignment. We call these exemplars "fast-lane companies." Each case study is also just One Page long.

Some of the exemplars are established companies, like Ford, Medtronic, and De Beers. Some are disrupters and pioneers, like Amazon, Netflix, and Tesla. Some are mid-market innovators, such as Bognet Construction, Valiant, and Basecamp.

We cover a wide range of industries, from car companies to chocolate manufacturers. Chicken restaurants to construction companies. CrossFit to Cirque du Soleil.

At the end of each chapter, I pose a few questions for your consideration. I call these questions "CHECKPOINTS." They are designed to help you evaluate how effectively your company is using that Accelerator.

I hope you enjoy reading the case studies as much as I enjoyed writing them.

"The task of leadership is to create an alignment of strengths, making our weaknesses irrelevant."

Peter Drucker
Professor
Claremont University

SPEED READING – ONE TEAM

In his landmark book, *Good to Great*, Jim Collins introduced the concept of "first who, then what."

So, let's start by clarifying your "who."

We believe that your corporate executive team is ultimately responsible for creating alignment. Therefore, Step One is for them to accept that responsibility.

This starts with your CEO. Your CEO must operate as the company's Chief Alignment Officer.

Randy Papadellis, the former CEO of the cranberry cooperative Ocean Spray, referred to himself as the "Chief Alignment Officer." Papadellis joined Ocean Spray in July 2000 as the Chief Operating Officer and was promoted to Chief Executive Officer in 2002. Here is how he described the transition,

"I believe the biggest difference between being CEO and COO is the job of alignment. When I became CEO, I realized very quickly that it was my responsibility to take the many constituencies we have in our business—our grower owners, our Board of Directors, our key suppliers, our key customers, or most importantly our employees—and make sure that they were aligned and moving in the same direction."

Aligned and moving in the same direction! My sentiments exactly.

Second, the entire corporate executive team must embrace alignment as a critical corporate initiative. There are several reasons for this:

- The corporate executive team is ultimately responsible for aligning the company's multiple divisions, departments, functions, and geographies.

- The corporate executive team is ultimately responsible for aligning the interests of the company's multiple stakeholders, including investors, creditors, employees, boards, vendors, customers, governments, the communities where you operate, and more. These stakeholders often have competing interests which must be aligned.

- The corporate executive team is ultimately responsible for aligning the company's multiple strategies, tactics, goals, priorities, and initiatives into a coherent corporate strategic plan (One Plan).

- The corporate executive team is ultimately responsible for aligning the company's resources—both human and financial—with the corporate strategy. Budgets must be allocated. Headcounts must be approved.

- Each corporate executive has the responsibility to align their functional area. The Chief Financial Officer must consolidate the budgets. The Chief Marketing Officer must integrate the marketing plans. The Chief Sales Officer must roll up the sales forecasts.

- Finally, the corporate team "sets the bar" for alignment. If they are not aligned as One Team, the rest of the organization will be dysfunctional. They must be role models for alignment. A misaligned executive team will never create an aligned company.

Let me say that again. A misaligned executive team will never create an aligned company.

While no team is perfect, in this chapter we will explore how Ford, The Carlyle Group, Berkshire Hathaway, and Valiant Integrated Services unleashed the accelerating power of alignment by working as One Team.

FORD

Alan Mulally was the CEO of Ford (NYSE: F) from September 2006 to June 2014.

During his tenure, Mulally led a highly successful alignment initiative called ONE FORD.

Perhaps more than any other exemplar we studied, the ONE FORD plan embodied the **Drive One Direction®** mindset. That is why it is our first One.

Besides, what better way to start the exemplars than with a car company that is driving in One Direction!

Mulally's turnaround of Ford is now legendary. Business "Hall of Fame" legendary.

The ONE FORD plan had several components that were so simple that Mulally had them printed on the back of business cards he would hand out. Here's what they said:

> ONE TEAM:
> People working together as a lean, global enterprise for automotive leadership, as measured by: Customer, Employee, Dealer, Investor, Supplier, Union/Council, and Community Satisfaction.
>
> ONE PLAN:
> Aggressively restructure to operate profitably at the current demand and changing model mix; Accelerate development of new products our customers want and value; Finance our plan and improve our balance sheet; Work together effectively as one team.
>
> ONE GOAL:
> An exciting viable Ford delivering profitable growth for all.

In addition, Mulally created sixteen "expected behaviors" that formed the basis of the cultural transformation. (See the More Resources section for the list.)

Mulally also instituted a new management process known as the Business Plan Review. Every Thursday, Ford's entire global leadership team was required to attend. This provided a very practical and hands-on way for Mulally to add management discipline to the ONE FORD plan.

"The expected behaviors and the Business Plan Review created the culture and management system to align everyone around a compelling vision, a comprehensive strategy, and a relentless implementation plan" said Mulally. "Everyone knew the plan, the status against that plan, and all the areas that needed special attention. Everyone was working together to change the reds to yellows to greens."

In 2014, *FORTUNE* magazine named Mulally the third best leader in the world, following Pope Francis and German Chancellor Angela Merkel.

The ONE FORD plan produced amazing results. During Mulally's tenure, Ford rebounded from a $12.7 billion loss in 2006 to a $6.3 billion pre-tax profit in 2014. The stock price roughly doubled during his 8 years as CEO and rose an astonishing 1,640 percent from the low during the financial crisis.

Does your executive team work as One Team?

THE CARLYLE GROUP

The Carlyle Group (NASDAQ: CG) is a global alternative asset manager with over 1,600 professionals operating in 31 offices around the world. They manage over $200B on behalf of over 1,925 investors from 90 countries.

Carlyle unleashed the accelerating power of alignment with their One Carlyle Culture.

At The Carlyle Group, alignment was built into the company by their three founders from Day One.

In fact, the One Carlyle Culture is a key component of how they deliver value to their customers. Glenn Youngkin, Carlyle's Co-CEO explains it this way, "Our professionals work together across product lines, sectors, and time zones to harness the knowledge, resources, and wisdom in our global operation to help create value for our investors."

"Carlyle has a culture of cooperation that is genetically embedded in the organization. If you look at our investment teams, we almost always have co-heads, not single heads. It is not a weird thing at Carlyle—in fact, it's the opposite," explained Kewsong Lee, Carlyle's other Co-CEO.

Obviously, this idea also was used when Carlyle appointed Glenn Youngkin and Kewsong Lee as the firm's Co-CEOs.

The private equity model has many virtues, but one foundational aspect is the alignment of interests.

Since the firm's inception, Carlyle professionals, Operating Executives, Senior Advisors, and other professionals have committed more than $11 billion of their own money alongside their fund investors. When an investment succeeds, everyone benefits. When an investment fails, everyone loses.

"We constantly work to break down the natural silos that might exist across funds, across countries, and across sectors. In the end, we are only as good as our people," explained Pete Clare, Carlyle's Co-Chief Investment Officer. "And we are better when we work together in the spirit of One Carlyle."

They also use recognition to reinforce their culture. Each year, the firm presents one employee in the world with the One Carlyle award, the highest honor that can be bestowed on an employee.

The Carlyle Group designed a culture of teamwork to deliver extraordinary value for its investors. Clearly, it has worked. The three founders are all billionaires.

Does your company have a One-Company culture?

BERKSHIRE HATHAWAY

Berkshire Hathaway (NYSE: BRK.B) is a multinational conglomerate holding company that owns 63 companies, from Acme Brick to the XTRA Corporation. The diversity of industries where they compete includes candy confectionery, retail, railroad, home furnishings, airlines, publishing, manufacturing, real estate, utilities, and more.

This eclectic mix of businesses is held together by One amazing Team.

Warren Buffett met Charlie Munger in 1959.

They have been business partners for six decades and have created billions in corporate and personal wealth.

"We've had so much fun in our partnership over the years," Buffett told CNBC in a joint interview with Munger, who called the partnership "almost hilarious, it's been so much fun."

Munger added they "don't agree totally on everything, and yet we're quite respectful of one another."

Buffett quipped that when they do disagree, Charlie says, "Well, you'll end up agreeing with me because you're smart and I'm right."

(I tried using this line with my wife, but it did not go over very well!)

Jim Collins made "getting the right people on the bus" part of the business lexicon. But the real issue is aligning all the bus drivers to work as One Team ... driving in One Direction. Fragmentation and infighting among the leadership team is one of the most caustic problems an organization can face. Yet, it is far too common.

Teamwork, alignment, and trust start at the top. The organization is never more aligned than the executive team.

But addressing executive team alignment issues will take courage. Skeletons will have to come out of the closet. Dysfunctional interpersonal relationships will need an intervention. People will have to address the conflicts they have been avoiding.

Someone will have to tell the emperor that he—or she—has no clothes.

Unfortunately, most executive teams never really deal with their misalignment issues.

Why? Because executives are afraid to speak their minds. Their need for self-preservation kicks in.

We see this all the time. We can tell that executives are holding something back. We can see their discomfort with the discussion or the decision that is about to be made. Yet, they are afraid to speak up.

Google just did a fascinating study about teams. They concluded that "psychological safety" was a key component of high-performance teams. It is this psychological safety that creates the environment for executive teams to have vigorous and candid debates about the company.

Psychological safety is the prerequisite to candor. And candor is the key to productive debates.

Creating psychological safety starts at the top. CEOs must create an environment where candor is valued, and opinions can be expressed without retribution.

How does your company's executive team resolve conflict?

VALIANT

Valiant Integrated Services (www.OneValiant.com) provides mission-critical services to the U.S. Department of Defense and intelligence communities, including our Joint Forces commands, the U.S. Army, Army National Guard, U.S. Navy, U.S. Marine Corps, U.S. Air Force, and coalition forces and has over 5,000 employees in over 20 countries across the globe.

Valiant was launched in February 2017 and certainly qualifies as a fast-lane company: they grew from zero to over $700M in fifteen months!

To build a company this fast, the executives had to quickly come together as One Team.

Valiant's impressive growth was fueled by three strategic acquisitions. In May 2017, they acquired selected assets of the Defense & Government Services business of the Supreme Group. In June 2017, they acquired ABM Government Services, and in May 2018, they acquired Cubic Global Defense Services.

While the press releases call them acquisitions, Valiant thinks of them as mergers. As Jim Jaska, Valiant's CEO explained, "You acquire groceries. You merge people."

For Valiant, alignment means blending three companies, with three different cultures, different brands, and different values into One Company. Of course, this starts with molding the executives into One Team.

There is a big difference between a group of executives and an executive team.

Groups of executives sit in the same room and present PowerPoint slides to each other. But people just pretend to listen and are probably checking email.

In contrast, high-performance executive teams have a shared vision, common goals, high accountability, and demonstrate a "we before me" attitude.

To help develop your executives into One Team, consider four factors: decisions, outputs, outcomes, and shared rewards.

- Decisions are the unique things that your executives decide *as a team*. In some companies, this list is actually quite small, since most of the decisions are made by individual executives without bringing the issue to the entire executive team.

- Outputs are the unique deliverables produced by your executives *as a team*. These include things like corporate strategy documents, annual budgets, or company goals.

- Outcomes are the unique results that your executive team is responsible for delivering *as a team*. These include things like corporate financial results, increasing shareholder value, or improving overall employee engagement.

- Shared rewards are the percentage of incentive compensation that executives earn *as a team*. At Valiant, each division is run by a Chief Operating Officer. To incentivize cross-divisional cooperation, 70 percent of each COO's incentive compensation is tied to corporate, not divisional, performance.

While Warren Buffett and Charlie Munger have been together for six decades, Valiant's executive team had to come together in six quarters. Jim Jaska has worked hard to make this happen, "When vision, objectives, and plans are shared, everyone works together to the benefit of the organization and the client."

Do your company's executives operate as a group or a team?

SUMMARY – ONE TEAM

We explored how fast-lane companies unleashed the accelerating power of alignment with One Team.

A misaligned executive team will <u>never</u> create an aligned company.

Alan Mulally unified and transformed Ford with his ONE FORD plan. The Carlyle Group leveraged their One Carlyle culture to create a competitive advantage. Warren Buffett and Charlie Munger have modeled teamwork for six decades. Jim Jaska had to build Valiant's executive team in just six quarters.

While each of these situations was radically different, each group of executives had to come together as One Team to drive their company in One Direction.

How about your company? Consider the following CHECKPOINTS to evaluate your executive team:

- Does your corporate executive team work as One Team?

- Does your CEO function as your Chief Alignment Officer?

- How long has your executive team been together?

- Does every executive have the same agenda?

- What percentage of executive compensation is tied to *corporate* results?

NOTE: To further evaluate the performance of your executive team, consider The Navigation Index™, a SHIFTPOINTS assessment based on the **Develop One Team** methodology.

ONE THING

"Deciding our One Thing has aligned our entire business around one simple, powerful strategy. Decisions are easier, our team is more engaged, and customers have become fans!"

MJ Wivell
Chief Executive Officer
BTI360

SPEED READING – ONE THING

Every company does lots of things.

Sadly, most never become truly great at anything.

For those of you who have not yet read my book, *Decide One Thing*, I will summarize it in One Sentence: you must be good at lots of things, but the way to win is to become differentiatingly great at One Thing.

In 1990, C.K. Prahalad and Gary Hamel introduced the idea of corporate competencies in a Harvard Business Review article entitled, "The Core Competence of the Corporation."

More recently, Strategy&, the strategy consulting arm of PwC, advised companies to develop a set of "differentiating capabilities." However, they do so with a word of caution:

> "Too many companies don't identify the few cross-functional capabilities they need to excel at in order to deliver on their value proposition. Not being clear about those capabilities, functions often decide to pursue functional excellence in silos. They strive to be world-class at everything they do, but often spread their resources too thin, and they don't excel at anything."

We strongly agree.

That is why we advise companies to pick ONE corporate competency and make it your One Thing.

Try to complete this sentence, "We are the best in the world at _____."

Most companies cannot honestly fill in that blank. After all, only One Company can be the best in the world.

However, *every* company can aspire to become the best in the world at something. So, every company can—and should—complete this sentence, "Our ambition is to become the best in the world at _____."

Step One is to choose something that your company could indeed become the best in the world at. And of course, there are many things that you can choose.

Step two is to align everyone—and everything—with your One Thing. After all, becoming the best in the world will require intense focus and disciplined investment. This is what turns your One Thing into a Differentiating Competitive Advantage.

We believe this is the most important component of creating alignment. Unfortunately, most companies do not have the discipline to Decide One Thing. That is why they can have visions, missions, values, and strategies … and still be massively misaligned.

Therefore, we strongly recommend that you lock this down before working on your vision, mission, values, strategy … or anything else.

In this chapter, we will explore how Dyson, Herman Miller, Ferrari, and BTI360 unleashed the accelerating power of alignment with an intense focus on One Thing.

DYSON

From its origins in a small workshop in rural England, Dyson (www.dyson.com) has grown into a technology company with a global footprint. They now employ over 8,500 people.

Dyson is good at lots of things, but they are differentiatingly great at engineering.

The Dyson website makes this crystal clear, "For us, engineering is everything." Or, in our language, engineering is their One Thing!

Not everyone at Dyson is an engineer, but they encourage everyone to think like one. And they are focused specifically on "transforming people's lives with our radical ideas, by solving the problems others ignore."

The story of Dyson is a testament to the irrational perseverance required to become differentiatingly great at something. It took James Dyson five years and 5,127 prototypes to perfect the Dual Cyclone™ technology that is at the core of the Dyson vacuum.

In 2007, Dyson created The James Dyson Award, an international award that inspires the next generation of design engineers. Each year, hundreds of engineers submit their designs.

In 2018, the grand prize went to Nicolas Orellana and Yaseen Noorani for their O-Wind Turbine, a 25cm sphere that converts wind into electricity. Other winners included a water-cleaning robot, a smartphone device to test for malaria, and a wheelchair designed for air travel.

In 2017, the company launched the Dyson Institute of Engineering and Technology in partnership with University of Warwick. Students work in a position at Dyson for four days a week, receive a salary, and have their tuition fees paid, allowing them to graduate debt free.

"These capable young engineers will be developing new technology alongside world-leading engineering practitioners, creating real products that end up in real homes—doing their academic work alongside their engineering projects." explained Dyson.

"Our philosophy remains the same as it was 25 years ago when James Dyson invented the first cyclonic vacuum cleaner. We remain family-owned. We don't bow to outside shareholders or report to the stock exchange. Instead we plot our own path, unshackled from conventional thinking."

James Dyson is driven to apply engineering to solve problems that other companies ignore. Perhaps that is why he is now Sir James Dyson, appointed to the rank of Knight Bachelor in 2007.

Is engineering your company's One Thing?

HERMAN MILLER

Herman Miller (NASDAQ: MLHR) is a manufacturer of office furniture, equipment, and home furnishings based in Zeeland, Michigan. Founded in 1905, the company has over 8,000 employees, over 600 dealers in 109 countries, and 33 Design Within Reach retail studios.

Their One Thing is perfectly clear: "design is a central part of our business."

Herman Miller's designs are part of museum collections worldwide. They have also received the Smithsonian Institution's Cooper Hewitt National Design Award and ranked Number One on *Contract Magazine's* list of "Brands that Inspire" for four straight years.

Some of the notable Herman Miller designers include Charles and Ray Eames, designers of the famous Eames lounge chair and ottoman; Isamu Noguchi, designer of the iconic Noguchi table; George Nelson, known as the father of American Modernism; and Bill Stumpf and Don Chadwick, designers of the Aeron, Embody, and Ergon office chairs.

A visit to the Herman Miller website features the profiles of dozens of other designers from all over the world.

In the last chapter, we learned that while not everyone at Dyson is an engineer, they encourage everyone to "think like one."

Herman Miller expresses the same idea, "You don't have to be a 'designer' to make things better—for customers, for the communities we do business in, and for a better world."

In addition to designing better furniture, Herman Miller is committed to designing better workspaces:

> "Organizations are struggling with the remnants of standardized workplaces, which only accommodate two broad categories of work—individual and

group—by providing two generic types of spaces—workstations and conference rooms. This type of floorplan cannot begin to support the diverse array of activities people do throughout the day.

It's clear that we need a more human-centered and diverse model for the workplace. And to implement this model, we need a more aligned process for designing and delivering the workplace—one where each stakeholder, from Facilities to HR to IT, is connected and involved from the outset."

They apply workspace design to improve organizational alignment!

Herman Miller is good at lots of things. Perhaps they are great at several things. But they are world-class at design.

Is design your company's One Thing?

FERRARI

Ferrari (NYSE: RACE) might be the ultimate fast-lane company.

When your stock ticker is RACE, you better be fast.

Ferrari began competing in the Formula One World Championship in 1950, the year the competition was established. Ferrari is the only constructor to have raced in every Formula One season—and they have won more championships than any other team.

Ferrari's One Thing is racing, and they put their money where their One Thing is.

Ferrari invests roughly $600M per year in their Formula One racing program. While the majority of this is recovered through sponsorships and Formula One's profit sharing, the net investment is believed to be in excess of $100M.

When you invest over One Hundred Million Dollars in one thing … it is your One Thing!

In 2003, they started Corse Clienti, which enables a small group of people to buy and race Ferrari Formula One cars. Here is how they describe the privilege, "Corse Clienti makes the car's owner feel like a real Scuderia *[Italian for "stable"]* Ferrari driver. Owners don't have to worry about anything except putting on their gloves and helmet, driving, and having fun, Corse Clienti does the rest."

In 2010, Ferrari also started the Ferrari Driver Academy to develop young Scuderia drivers. "I'd like to think that Ferrari can create drivers as well as cars," explained Enzo Ferrari.

A recent trip to a Ferrari store was a testament to the amazing power of Ferrari's investment in racing.

The store's prominent feature was a red (of course) Ferrari Formula One car on display. The store sold T-shirts, scale models of Ferrari cars, Ferrari sneakers, Ferrari hats, Ferrari luggage, Ferrari gloves, Ferrari pens, Ferrari sunglasses, Ferrari flags, and more.

There is even a children's section that sold Ferrari onesies, Ferrari baby shoes, and all sorts of other items to indoctrinate your child into the faithful.

Several years ago, I was in Italy on the weekend of the Formula One race at Monza, Italy—the home of Ferrari. The Ferrari Scuderia won the race, and the entire nation went wild.

Very few brands achieve iconic status. Fewer still achieve the kind of fanatical evangelicalism among their customers that Ferrari does. And the most fascinating thing about Ferrari is that most of its passionate fans will never own one of their cars. (They only sell 9,000 cars per year!)

Think about that. How many people who will never be your customers are nonetheless fanatical ambassadors for your brand?

For Ferrari, it all starts with racing.

Is speed your One Thing?

BTI360

BTI360 (www.bti360.com) is a rapidly growing software development firm that works with government clients.

They create alignment—and a Differentiating Competitive Advantage—with an intense focus on One Thing.

BTI360 provides their software development as a subcontractor to a large prime contractor. However, over three hundred other companies are on that same subcontract.

So, how do you stand out when you have 299 competitors that look alike, sound alike, and essentially provide the exact same service?

BTI360 decided that they could become differentiatingly great at "developing ultimate teammates." This led to phrases like "software development is a team sport" that are a key part of their unique culture.

Thus, "developing ultimate teammates" became their One Thing.

MJ Wivell, their co-founder and CEO, says it this way, "Most companies use people to build the business. We use the business to build people."

BTI360 then applied our *"Decide One Thing, Align Everything, Win!®"* model to align everything in their company.

"Once we found our One Thing, decision-making became very easy," said Jeremy Nimtz, BTI360's co-founder. "We would simply evaluate everything with one simple question, 'Will this help us become differentiatingly great at our One Thing?'"

Since going through the Decide One Thing process, BTI360 has experienced amazing results. The company has quadrupled in size and has won eight—and counting—Best Place to Work awards.

I am (obviously) biased, but I think that aligning your entire company with the strategy of becoming world-class great at One Thing is one of the best models.

Customers may not care about your vision. Or your mission. Or your values.

But they will flock to a company that is world-class great at solving One of their problems.

Is developing people your One Thing?

P.S. BTI360 calls people teammates, not employees, which is exactly what you would expect from an organization that puts people first.

SUMMARY – ONE THING

If all you do is decide One Thing, it does not do anything.

But if you align everyone—and everything—with your One Thing, amazing things happen.

Since applying the *Decide One Thing, Align Everything, Win!®* model, our best client has quintupled in size. Several have doubled. One is in the Inc. 500 Hall of Fame.

While not everyone at Dyson is an engineer, they encourage everyone to think like one. At Herman Miller, designers are the rock stars. Ferrari invests over One Hundred Million Dollars in their One Thing. BTI360 is in the business of developing software, but their One Thing is developing ultimate teammates.

How about your company? Surely, you are very good at many things. Perhaps you are great at a few things. But are you really, truly world-class great at anything?

Consider the following CHECKPOINTS to evaluate your company's One Thing:

- What are your company's core competencies?

- Which One is the most important One?

- Does your company invest disproportionately in that One?

- Are you already great at your One Thing? If not, what will it take to become the best in the world at it?

- Complete this sentence: "We are good at lots of things, but our ambition is to become the best in the world at _____."

ONE VISION

"There is a big difference between being an organization with a vision statement and becoming a truly visionary organization. The difference lies in creating alignment ..."

Jim Collins
Author
Good to Great

SPEED READING – ONE VISION

Every company has a vision.

But most of them are pretty blurry.

Only 35 percent of adults have 20/20 vision, and an even smaller percentage of companies do.

Most companies suffer from some sort of vision disorder, such as myopia—where they can't focus on the long-term, or tunnel vision—where they get blindsided by market shifts and discontinuities.

Worse yet, according to Achievers' 2015 North America Workforce report, a whopping 60 percent of employees did not know their company's vision.

Fast-lane companies create alignment by having just One Vision. After all, how can you create One Company when every division has a different vision?

While it is critical to have One Vision, there are many ways to articulate one. In fact, we discovered four common ways:

- The "visionary" vision

- The "inspiring" vision

- The "company ambition" vision

- The "Big Hairy Audacious Goal (BHAG)" vision

In fast-lane companies, the process of defining the vision is as important as the vision itself. They use a collaborative process that combines top-down aspirations with bottom-up forecasts.

Assumptions are debated. Competitors are studied. Trends are extrapolated.

Of course, smart companies do a gut check before launching the vision. They understand what it will really take to turn the vision into reality. They have "counted the costs."

There is nothing more demoralizing to a company than a unilateral, top-down vision that is more of a delusional pipe-dream than a vision.

And finally, high-performers make the case for the vision. Every executive—not just the CEO—can passionately articulate the vision and can explain *why* this is your vision.

Of all the visions you could have chosen, why did you select this One? If you can't answer that question, no one will buy in.

In this chapter, we will examine how Virgin Hyperloop One, Habitat for Humanity, Southwest Airlines, and Mothers Against Drunk Driving unleashed the accelerating power of alignment with their unique, One-of-a-Kind Visions.

VIRGIN HYPERLOOP ONE

Virgin Hyperloop One (www.hyperloop-one.com) is a
California-based transportation innovator.

*Elon Musk unleashed the global hyperloop revolution with
One Paper.*

The problem with most visions is that they are not
particularly visionary.

In contrast, the vision articulated for the hyperloop by Elon
Musk, of Tesla and SpaceX fame, is an exemplar.

The origin of Musk's vision—like all world-changing
visions—was an extreme dissatisfaction with the status quo.
In this case, Musk was dissatisfied with the Caltrain high-
speed rail (HSR) proposal to "modernize" the rail service
between San Francisco and Los Angeles.

Musk wrote a 58-page paper—imagine a college physics
term paper written by a billionaire CEO—outlining his vision
for a radically better way to modernize and accelerate travel
between San Francisco and Los Angeles.

He also had the audacity to suggest that his hyperloop
vision would revolutionize travel worldwide in the same way
he was revolutionizing the automobile industry with Tesla
and the space industry with SpaceX.

"Sci-fi writers and dreamers have long envisioned ways to
travel at high speeds through low-pressure tubes. Rocketry
pioneer Robert Goddard in 1909 proposed a vacuum train
very similar in concept to the Hyperloop. In 1972, the RAND
Corp. conceived a supersonic underground railway called
the Vactrain. The idea was waiting for the right combination
of talent, technology, and business case to become a
reality."

In August 2014, ten months after Musk published his paper, Hyperloop One was started in a Los Angeles garage to commercialize Musk's vision.

In May 2016, Hyperloop One launched a "global challenge" that was an "open call to individuals, universities, companies and governments to develop comprehensive proposals for using Hyperloop One's disruptive transport technology in their region to move passengers and freight point-to-point, swiftly, and on-demand."

The Hyperloop One Global Challenge yielded 2,600 registrants in five months.

Elon Musk wrote One Paper. It launched what may be the most transformational change in transportation in years.

Thousands of people and millions of venture capital dollars aligned behind Musk's vision. To them, it was an inspiring purpose worth investing their lives—and their money—to accomplish.

Does your company have a visionary vision?

NOTE: In February 2018, the state of California cancelled the "high-speed" rail program after extensive cost overruns and schedule delays.

HABITAT FOR HUMANITY

Habitat for Humanity® (www.habitat.org) is a global nonprofit housing organization working in all 50 states in the U.S. and in approximately 70 countries around the world.

Habitat envisions "a world where everyone has a decent place to live."

Millard and Linda Fuller co-founded Habitat for Humanity in 1976. What began as a grassroots effort on a community farm in southern Georgia has evolved into a global organization that has helped more than 22 million people.

In 1996, former U.S. President Bill Clinton awarded Millard Fuller the Presidential Medal of Freedom—the nation's highest civilian honor—calling Habitat "...the most successful continuous community service project in the history of the United States."

Habitat homeowners help build their own homes alongside volunteers. In 2018, more than 1.4 million people volunteered with Habitat, helping families achieve the strength, stability, and self-reliance they need to build better lives for themselves.

"With a little help, we all have the potential to stand on our own," explained Habitat CEO Jonathan Reckford. "It is an incredible experience to help homeowners build or improve a place to live and see how they are then able to build a better life for themselves and their families."

Surveys of Habitat homeowners show improved grades, better financial health, and parents who are more confident that they can meet their family's needs.

Providing "a decent place to live" provides the solid foundation for all of this.

While Habitat has been wildly successful, the need is still great. Over 1.6 billion people in the world do not have adequate shelter, and 100 million more have no home at all.

While 2018 was a record year for Habitat, Jonathan Reckford put their success in perspective, "We have millions of reasons to celebrate, and millions more to keep building toward a world where everyone has a decent place to live."

Maintaining focus is challenging for every company … but it is especially challenging for nonprofits. Most suffer from mission creep. After all, it is extremely difficult to say "no" to a pressing humanitarian need.

Habitat is intensely focused on housing. They are world-class great at it. I commend them for having the discipline to say "no" to thousands of good ideas so they can say "yes" to the best One(s).

At Habitat, the vision is not just a static statement printed on coffee mugs. Their vision provides an ongoing and dynamic perspective that keeps everyone—and everything—aligned.

Does your company have an inspiring vision?

SOUTHWEST AIRLINES

Southwest Airlines (NYSE: LUV) began in 1971 as a low-cost carrier with three airplanes flying to three cities in Texas. Now, they have approximately 750 airplanes making more than 4,000 weekday departures during peak travel seasons to over nearly 100 destinations. More than 58,000 employees serve over 120 million passengers every year.

Southwest is a great example of a company whose vision statement clearly articulates their ambition.

In January 2013, Southwest launched a new vision: to become the world's most loved, most flown, and most profitable airline.

Their vision has three components, and each can be measured.

The "**most loved**" component expresses how they want people—customers, employees, partners, suppliers, and investors—to feel about them. Here is how they are doing:

- Southwest has been #1 in the DOT Consumer Satisfaction Ranking for 23 of the last 27 years.

- Southwest is ranked #2 on the list of Top-Rated Workplaces in 2018 by Indeed.

- Southwest received 301,825 resumes and hired 6,275 new employees in 2017.

Since launching their vision, the stock is up more than 300 percent!

The "**most flown**" component expresses their desire to be the biggest. Here is how they are doing:

- Southwest is America's largest domestic airline in terms of originating domestic passengers with 24 percent market share at the end of 2017.

The "**most profitable**" component can also be quantified. Here is how they are doing:

- In 2017, they celebrated 45 consecutive years of profitability.

While Southwest calls it a "vision statement," perhaps it should be called an "ambition statement." It has three simple components, which makes it easy to understand. Each can be measured, which makes it easy for them to evaluate their progress.

In addition to their vision, Southwest also has a mission statement, a set of core values, and a purpose—to connect people to what's important in their lives through friendly, reliable, and low-cost air travel. All of these elements work together to unleash the accelerating power of alignment.

By any measure, Southwest is an amazing company. For the 24th consecutive year, they were named to FORTUNE's 2018 list of "World's Most Admired Companies." This is just one of many accolades and awards.

Does your vision statement articulate your company's ambition?

MOTHERS AGAINST DRUNK DRIVING

Mothers Against Drunk Driving (www.MADD.com) is a Washington, D.C., nonprofit organization with over 400 employees, over 8,000 volunteers, and over 200 field locations.

It all started with One Mom.

Candace Lightner founded Mothers Against Drunk Driving on September 5, 1980, after her 13-year-old daughter, Cari, was killed by a drunk driver.

In the nearly 40 years since their founding, drunk driving deaths have been reduced by 50%.

While that is impressive, they are intensely focused on One Number: zero.

Zero deaths. Zero injuries. Zero families impacted by impaired driving.

Here is how they bring their vision to life, "At MADD, we believe in zero. Zero fathers who aren't there for bedtime. Zero mothers who miss the first day of kindergarten. Zero sons and daughters who never come home. We believe in zero victims of drunk driving. Since MADD's founding, we've made great strides … but it is not good enough because every year, drunk driving injures over 290,000 people. It's not good enough because every year, drunk driving takes 10,000 lives. It's not good enough because it isn't zero."

MADD's campaign to get to zero has four strategic initiatives:

- High-visibility law enforcement, including DUI checkpoints.
- Ignition interlocks for all convicted drunk drivers, which forces offenders to provide a sober breath sample before operating their vehicles.

- Advanced vehicle technology, including autonomous vehicles which have the potential to eliminate roadway fatalities.
- Public support, since everyone has a responsibility to help eliminate drunk driving.

In *Built to Last*, Jim Collins and Jerry Porras introduced the concept of the Big, Hairy, Audacious Goal or BHAG (pronounced bee-hag). Here is how they describe it, "A true BHAG is clear and compelling, serves as unifying focal point of effort, and acts as a clear catalyst for team spirit. It has a clear finish line, so the organization can know when it has achieved the goal; people like to shoot for finish lines."

MADD's "zero" is a brilliant example of a BHAG. It is clear, simple, and inspiring.

It is also a brilliant example of the One Number strategy. When you can summarize your vision in One Number, everyone knows exactly how you keep score.

Lots of numbers are important, but it is the job of the leader to define which One is the most important.

Revenue. Revenue Growth. Profitability. Market Share. Customer Satisfaction. Net Promoter. Earnings per Share. Share Price. All of these (and more) are good numbers.

Which One is the most important? That depends on how you define success. Ideally, find One Number that is simple to measure and simple to communicate.

MADD's vision is One Word that also happens to be One Number. Brilliant!

If you had to summarize your vision with One Number, what would it be?

SUMMARY – ONE VISION

There are many ways to articulate a vision.

If you want to improve alignment, it is essential that you have just One.

Elon Musk wrote a visionary 58-page paper that started a transportation revolution. Habitat has a visionary vision. Southwest wants to be number One. MADD has a visionary BHAG that is just One Word … and One Number.

And remember, just because a company has One Vision does not automatically mean that everyone—and everything—is aligned with it.

How about your company? Consider the following CHECKPOINTS to evaluate your company's corporate vision:

- Does your company have One—and Only One— Vision?

- Is it a visionary vision, an inspiring vision, an ambition, or a BHAG?

- Has it been codified as a vision statement?

- Is it clear, compelling, unifying, inspiring, and differentiating?

- Does everyone in your company understand the vision?

ONE
MISSION

"There is an increasing awareness that the purpose of a company has to be beyond shareholder value, and that this is not something that will cost your business but something that will enhance your business."

Michael Beer
Professor
Harvard Business School

SPEED READING – ONE MISSION

Your company has a mission.

Otherwise, you should not exist.

As best as I can determine, the term "mission statement" first appeared in an obscure U.S. Department of Commerce document published in 1960. Since then, it has become conventional wisdom to suggest that companies should have One.

While every company has a mission, our research revealed that many—but certainly not all—companies have mission statements.

Crafting a corporate mission statement can be an excruciating process.

In 1983, Bain and Company, the management consulting firm, embarked on the process of crafting a mission statement. The senior partners of the firm spent *five days* holed up in a cabin in New Hampshire. They agonized over every word and ultimately crafted this statement:

> "We help our clients create such high levels of value that together we set new standards of excellence in our respective industries."

Bill Bain, their founder and CEO, described it this way, "This is the combination of those things that we already do when we are at our best and those things that we need to do to be at our best more often."

While most of the mission statements we reviewed were vanilla and uninspiring, a well-crafted One—like Bain's—can help companies create alignment.

In this chapter, we will look at how fast-lane companies addressed this issue. Amazon's mission is internally focused and articulates what they aspire to become. Tesla's mission is externally focused and describes what they aspire to do.

To me, aspirations are visions, not missions, but who am I to argue with Jeff Bezos and Elon Musk?

Next, we will look at Medtronic. They have been guided by their mission for sixty years!

Finally, we will explore One.org and learn how companies can make their mission more inspiring.

Of course, it is not enough to have One Mission; you must use your mission to guide both big strategic decisions and everyday tactics. You must align everyone—and everything—with it. You must prune things that are not aligned with your mission.

AMAZON

Amazon (NASDAQ: AMZN) started out selling books. Now, it sells everything.

Amazon keeps the vast enterprise aligned with One Obsession.

Jeff Bezos has built Amazon into one of the most successful and transformational companies in history. And on October 27, 2017, he became the richest person in the world.

So, what was the secret to Amazon's amazing success?

When Amazon.com launched in 1995, their mission was "to be Earth's most customer-centric company, where customers can find and discover anything they might want to buy online, and endeavors to offer its customers the lowest possible prices."

In one of Bezos' annual letters, he describes it this way, "There are many ways to center a business. You can be competitor focused, you can be product focused, you can be technology focused, you can be business model focused, and there are more. But in my view, obsessive customer focus is by far the most protective of Day 1 vitality."

Let's unpack this statement.

First, Bezos is obviously right. There are indeed many ways to center a business. In other words, there are many ways to align a business.

Second, Bezos presents the options as discreet choices. His implication is that your company must choose One of them. Do you agree?

Third, Bezos bridges from describing the other choices as "focused" to Amazon having "obsessive customer focus."

"Obsessive" is an extreme word. In extreme cases, obsession can become a dysfunctional pathology.

Perhaps "obsessive customer focus" sounds extreme. But clearly, it has worked for Amazon.

Unfortunately, most companies are distracted, divided, and dysfunctional. Many others are obsessed with the wrong things.

Developing One Obsession is a tremendous way to improve strategic alignment. You will just have to agree on what to become obsessed with.

Finally, while becoming "the Earth's most customer-centric company" was indeed Amazon's original mission, they now describe it as one of the fourteen leadership principles that make up their DNA.

If you are inspired to copy Amazon's example, complete this sentence: "Our mission is to become the most _____-obsessed company in the world."

TESLA

In July 2016, Tesla (NASDAQ: TSLA) updated their mission statement.

They changed One Word.

The original mission was to "accelerate the world's transition to sustainable transport."

The new one is to "accelerate the world's transition to sustainable energy."

Here's why they made the change. On August 1, 2016, Tesla agreed to acquire SolarCity, the largest solar provider in America.

Here is how Tesla explained the case for the acquisition,

"We would be the world's only vertically integrated energy company offering end-to-end clean energy products to our customers. This would start with the car that you drive and the energy that you use to charge it, and would extend to how everything else in your home or business is powered. With your Model S, Model X, or Model 3, your solar panel system, and your Powerwall all in place, you would be able to deploy and consume energy in the most efficient and sustainable way possible, lowering your costs and minimizing your dependence on fossil fuels and the grid."

Tesla has a big mission and has a big strategy to make it happen.

To ramp production to 500,000 cars per year, Tesla alone would have consumed the entire worldwide supply of lithium-ion batteries. Therefore, they built the Gigafactory (the name comes from the word "giga," the unit of measurement representing "billions.") Once complete, Tesla expects the Gigafactory to be the biggest building in the world—and it will be powered entirely by renewable energy sources.

One of the key aspects of the **Drive One Direction®** model is the concept of "Aligned Agility." We want companies to be both highly aligned and extremely agile. The fact that Tesla could pivot the entire company and integrate a major strategic acquisition by simply changing One Word in their mission statement is a testament to their agility.

As you might expect, Elon Musk, the CEO of Tesla, has a fascinating way to describe alignment, "Every person in your company is a vector. Your progress is determined by the sum of all vectors."

For those of you who did not get that, you might want to brush up on your linear algebra.

Tesla is a mission-driven company. By simply changing One Word, they were able to integrate Tesla Motors and Solar City.

Two companies with One (BIG) Mission.

Does your company have a mission ... or a BIG One?

MEDTRONIC

Medtronic (NYSE: MDT) develops therapies that treat nearly 70 conditions, including some of the world's most challenging chronic diseases such as diabetes, obesity, cancer, and heart disease. They have revenues in excess of $30B, operate in more than 160 countries, and have over 86,000 employees.

They keep everything aligned with their "One Company. One Mission." framework.

This amazing success story started in a garage in 1949 in Minneapolis, Minnesota. (And you thought that only happened in Silicon Valley!)

Normally, we advise companies that their mission statement should be just One Sentence. Otherwise, no one will remember what it is.

Medtronic's mission statement, in contrast, has six sentences, multiple clauses, and is over 170 words long. While this violates our penchant for brevity, I must give them credit for longevity.

Their mission statement was written by their late founder, Earl Bakken, in 1960. They spent a few years locking it down and they have used it verbatim ever since.

THE MEDTRONIC MISSION

1. To contribute to human welfare by application of biomedical engineering in the research, design, manufacture, and sale of instruments or appliances that alleviate pain, restore health, and extend life.

2. To direct our growth in the areas of biomedical engineering where we display maximum strength and ability; to gather people and facilities that tend to augment these areas; to continuously build on these areas through education and knowledge

assimilation; to avoid participation in areas where we cannot make unique and worthy contributions.

3. To strive without reserve for the greatest possible reliability and quality in our products; to be the unsurpassed standard of comparison and to be recognized as a company of dedication, honesty, integrity, and service.

4. To make a fair profit on current operations to meet our obligations, sustain our growth, and reach our goals.

5. To recognize the personal worth of employees by providing an employment framework that allows personal satisfaction in work accomplished, security, advancement opportunity, and means to share in the company's success.

6. To maintain good citizenship as a company.

When you stay with One Mission for six decades, it is easy for everyone to align with it, "Nothing I can say about Medtronic today makes me happier or more optimistic about the future than the fact that the Mission is deeply embedded as a permanent part of the culture," explained Earl Bakken.

Will your company have the discipline to stay with One Mission for six decades?

ONE.ORG

So, perhaps you are thinking that your company could never be a Medtronic. Your purpose will never be as inspiring as saving lives.

One Way to align everyone is to create a nonprofit or foundation as your One.org.

Today's workforce needs to be inspired.

To stay aligned with my One Theme, I thought it would be nice to profile ONE, the international organization cofounded by Bono from the band U2. ONE is focused on ending extreme poverty and preventable disease, particularly in Africa.

The ONE name was inspired by the belief that One Voice, coming together with many others, could change the world for the better.

And I'd like to challenge you to believe that One Company—yours—could also come together to change the world for the better.

For example, many companies have created their own nonprofit or foundation, often using the .org domain extension as part of the brand. This becomes a secondary corporate structure that complements their for-profit business.

For example, Salesforce created Salesforce.org. Here is how they describe the impact, "Over the last 18 years, Salesforce.org has become a vital part of the Salesforce culture—and has allowed us to engage our employees in their communities and support the effectiveness of the social sector."

Salesforce is also one of the leaders in a corporate philanthropy movement called "Pledge 1%." This challenges companies to give 1% of equity, 1% of employees' time, 1%

of products, and/or 1% of profits to philanthropic endeavors. Over 8,500 companies have now taken the pledge.

Since their founding, Salesforce has given more than $260 million in grants, donated 3.8 million hours of community service, and provided product donations for more than 40,000 nonprofits and higher education institutions.

Of course, there are other ways to align your company with an inspiring purpose.

In fact, the best companies find a way to align their corporate philanthropy with their core competency.

David Abney, the CEO of UPS, explains it this way, "We focus on areas where our volunteer efforts and philanthropy not only make a difference, but also where they align with our vision, which is to 'connect a global community through intelligent logistics networks.'"

Of course, you could always adopt an existing corporate charity. Perhaps you should consider Bono's ONE.

Does your company have One Cause that you support as part of a "we give back" culture?

SUMMARY – ONE MISSION

One of my favorite taglines is used by Kashi, the organic food company. They are "seven whole grains on a mission."

If seven whole grains can be on a mission, then so can you!

Amazon built one of the world's greatest companies with their customer obsession. Tesla is on a mission to accelerate the world's transition to sustainable energy. Medtronic has saved millions of lives with theirs. Many companies are using a .org to make their mission more inspiring.

How about your company? Consider the following CHECKPOINTS to evaluate your company's mission:

- Does your company have One—and Only One—Mission?

- Is it clear, compelling, unifying, inspiring, and differentiating?

- Is everyone—and everything—aligned with it?

- Is it passionately and consistently communicated?

- Do you say "no" to things that are not aligned with your mission?

"In many organizations, people are literally pushing in different directions, making the net effect zero. When you can get everyone moving together, it creates greater performance at the organizational level. I think the future of work is going to focus on how to align people."

Stewart Butterfield
Chief Executive Officer
Slack

SPEED READING – ONE CODE

Every company has values.

But most struggle to make them more than just words on posters.

According to Wikipedia, a value system is "a set of consistent ethic values and measures used for the purpose of ethical or ideological integrity. A well-defined value system is a moral code."

Most—but certainly not all—of the companies we studied had a codified list of core values.

Unfortunately, core values can also be a source of cynicism. Sadly, several CEOs we interviewed did not have their company's values memorized. Dozens of employees shared stories of executives whose behaviors were in direct violation of their company's values. Perhaps millions have been impacted by other forms of corporate hypocrisy.

Despair.com has built a very nice business selling posters mocking core values. Here are a few examples:

- Perseverance: The courage to ignore the obvious wisdom of turning back.

- Procrastination: Hard work pays off over time, but laziness always pays off now.

- Mediocrity: It takes a lot less time and most people won't notice the difference until it's too late.

Unfortunately, Gallup's research revealed that only 23 percent of employees know how to apply their company's values to their work. Nonetheless, we included core values as one of the Accelerators because many exemplar companies used them effectively to create alignment. Some of the common best practices include:

- They codified their values into One integrated value system. We call this your One Code.

- They passionately communicate the values, so everyone knows what they are.

- The employees—especially the senior executives—live them, breathe them, and personify them.

- They only hire people who share their values, and never tolerate behavior that violates them.

- They infuse their values into every fiber of the company, aligning every process, guiding every decision.

- They reward and recognize people who demonstrate their values.

- They justify them, so everyone knows WHY these are the values.

- They translate their values into a set of expected behaviors. (Netflix calls this their "Culture Code.")

Core values can't be seen on the balance sheet, but they can be one of your company's most valuable assets. They can allow a company to withstand a crisis. They can guide leaders faced with radically complex decisions.

Assuming they are more than just words on posters in the break room.

In this chapter, we will explore how Blommer Chocolate, Hilton, the Mayo Clinic, and Netflix codified their values to unleash the accelerating power of alignment.

BLOMMER CHOCOLATE

The Blommer Chocolate Company (www.blommer.com) is the largest cocoa processor and ingredient chocolate supplier in North America.

Blommer unleashed the accelerating power of alignment with One DNA.

Blommer Chocolate was founded in 1939 in Chicago, Illinois, by three brothers; Henry, Al, and Bernard. For almost 80 years, the Blommer family has run the company.

The company now has over 800 employees, including the third generation of Blommers: Peter, Rick and Steve Blommer, Peter Drake, and Tori Blommer-O'Malley.

(Although these Blommer family members come from different branches of the family tree, they still share some common DNA. This could actually be confirmed by Autosomal DNA testing, which measures the number and length of common DNA segments.)

Peter Blommer, the grandson of Henry, started working for the company in 1991 in the Union City, California, plant. He became the President and Chief Executive Officer in 2009.

To manage the rapidly expanding company, Peter needed to recruit and incorporate outside executives who were not part of the Blommer family but shared the company's DNA.

After all, your company's DNA—just like your personal DNA—defines who you are and differentiates you from everyone else.

Here is how Peter Blommer described it, "Our unique company DNA is a function of several factors, including our history as a family business, our company values, our philosophy of management, and more. Creating company-wide alignment with the Blommer DNA was a top priority when I became CEO."

At this point, roughly three-quarters of the senior management team is comprised of executives from outside the family.

The results from Blommer's investments in strategic alignment have been sweet. (Pardon the pun.) The business continues to grow, the family relationships are healthier than ever, and the company is positioned to thrive for generations to come.

Your company may not be a family business, but that does not mean you can't run it like one. You can treat your employees like family. You can treat your customers like family. You can even treat your vendors like family.

Of course, this means that you must codify your company's unique DNA.

Do your values emanate from the founder's DNA?

HILTON HOTELS

Hilton (NYSE: HLT) is a global hospitality company with a portfolio of seventeen brands, 5,700 properties, and over 923,000 rooms.

Hilton improved alignment by creating One List of core values.

Perhaps you are thinking, "Of course they have One List of values." However, this was not always the case.

When Christopher Nassetta took over as CEO in 2007, he discovered that Hilton had over *thirty different lists* of core values.

Here is how he described the process of consolidating them into One List:

"We did a lot of work with teams around the world, and asked people to look at all their values statements and boil them down. Then we took all those ideas with us on a two-day offsite with about 12 of us. There was a lot of overlap, and we tried to consolidate it. What I ended up saying to them was, let's use some of our own skills and brand it, not because I want to be cute about it, but because people will remember it. I started looking around the room and at the letters and they came together as HILTON—H for hospitality, I for integrity, L for leadership, T for teamwork, O for ownership and N for now. To reinforce them, we are constantly referring to the letters—in newsletters, in town halls—almost to the point where we are driving people crazy. But it works."

For your reference, here is the One List of Hilton values:

- **HOSPITALITY**—We're passionate about delivering exceptional guest experiences.

- **INTEGRITY**—We do the right thing, all the time.

- **L**EADERSHIP—We're leaders in our industry and in our communities.

- **T**EAMWORK—We're team players in everything we do.

- **O**WNERSHIP—We're the owners of our actions and decisions.

- **N**OW—We operate with a sense of urgency and discipline.

As you can see, each value has both One Word and an expected behavior. This extra step turns static values into a dynamic corporate code that can drive behavior.

Of course, this starts with having One List.

Does your company have One—and Only One—List of core values?

MAYO CLINIC

The Mayo Clinic has over 4,700 physicians and scientists. Like many companies, they have a list of core values.

But they are crystal clear about which one is Number One.

In 1863, Dr. William Mayo opened a private medical practice in Rochester, Minnesota. His sons, William and Charles, continued to build the practice around a relatively innovative concept at the time—hiring a diverse staff of specialists to work as an integrated team. Their model produced better health outcomes and quickly began drawing patients from around the world.

The Mayo Clinic's core values "are an expression of the vision and intent of our founders, the original Mayo physicians and the Sisters of Saint Francis." There are eight of them:

1. RESPECT—Treat everyone in our diverse community, including patients, their families and colleagues, with dignity.

2. INTEGRITY—Adhere to the highest standards of professionalism, ethics and personal responsibility, worthy of the trust our patients place in us.

3. COMPASSION—Provide the best care, treating patients and family members with sensitivity and empathy.

4. HEALING—Inspire hope and nurture the well-being of the whole person, respecting physical, emotional and spiritual needs.

5. TEAMWORK—Value the contributions of all, blending the skills of individual staff members in unsurpassed collaboration.

6. INNOVATION—Infuse and energize the organization, enhancing the lives of those we serve, through the creative ideas and unique talents of each employee.

7. EXCELLENCE—Deliver the best outcomes and highest quality service through the dedicated effort of every team member.

8. STEWARDSHIP—Sustain and reinvest in our mission and extended communities by wisely managing our human, natural and material resources.

However, they specifically identify One Value as their primary value: The needs of the patient come first.

Elevating One Value to be Number One makes things incredibly clear. It takes courage and discipline, since every value is important.

It has worked for Mayo. In 2018 over 1.3 million people from 136 countries went to the Mayo Clinic for care, and in the latest U.S. News & World Report rankings, the Mayo Clinic is the Number One hospital overall and Number One in more specialties than any other hospital in the nation.

What is your company's Number One Value?

NETFLIX

Netflix (NASDAQ: NFLX) is the world's leading internet entertainment service with over 109 million members.

They unleashed the accelerating power of alignment with a very unique Culture Code.

In 2009, Netflix' CEO Reed Hastings, Chief Talent Officer Patti McCord, and a few others collaborated to create a 127-slide presentation about the culture they wanted to create.

Since it was posted online in 2009, the Netflix's "Culture Code" deck has been viewed more than 10 million times. Sheryl Sandberg, the Chief Operating Officer of Facebook, described it as one of the most important documents to ever come out of Silicon Valley. (The current version is now a long text page on their corporate website.)

Many of their ideas are antithetical to the traditional HR approach. Their vacation policy is, "Take vacation." Their expense policy is five words long: "Act in Netflix's best interests."

Another unique aspect is "the keeper test" that managers use to evaluate employees: "If one of your employees told you he or she was leaving for a job at a peer company, would you fight hard to keep that employee at Netflix? If the answer is 'no,' then Netflix will move that person out of the business. Sustained B-level performance, despite 'A for effort', generates a generous severance package, with respect."

Perhaps most interesting is their approach to alignment, which they describe as "Highly Aligned, Loosely Coupled." Here is how they explain it:

> As companies grow, they often become highly centralized and inflexible. Symptoms include:

- Senior management is involved in tons of small decisions

- There are numerous cross-departmental buy-in meetings to socialize tactics

- Pleasing other internal groups takes precedence over pleasing customers

- The organization is highly coordinated and less prone to error, but slow and frustrating

  We avoid this by being highly aligned and loosely coupled. We spend lots of time debating strategy together, and then trust each other to execute on tactics without prior approvals. Often, two groups working on the same goals won't know of, or have approval over, their peer activities. If, later, the activities don't seem right, we have a candid discussion. We may find that the strategy was too vague or the tactics were not aligned with the agreed strategy. And we discuss generally how we can do better in the future.

  The success of a "Highly Aligned, Loosely Coupled" work environment is dependent upon the collaborative efforts of high-performance individuals and effective context. Ultimately, the end goal is to grow the business for bigger impact while increasing flexibility and agility. We seek to be big, fast, and nimble.

Netflix's unique approach to alignment has produced stunning results. Since publishing the culture deck in 2009, Netflix has grown nearly tenfold!

Does your company have a radically unique corporate code?

SUMMARY – ONE CODE

Your corporate values can be one of the your most valuable assets.

Assuming that they are not just words on posters.

Blommer Chocolate is a family business that quite literally started with One DNA. Hilton consolidated multiple lists of values into One—and Only One—List. The Mayo Clinic did more than just make a list … they selected One Value to be their primary One. Netflix chose to articulate their values in a 127-slide presentation.

How about your company? Consider the following CHECKPOINTS to evaluate your company's One Code:

- Does your company have One—and Only One—List of values?

- Can you explain why you chose them (and why you did not choose others)?

- Are they clear, compelling, inspiring, unifying, and differentiating?

- Is alignment (or one of its many synonyms) one of your values?

- What does your company do to make them more than just words on posters?

"A brand is a singular idea or concept that you own inside the mind of a prospect."

Al Ries
Author
Differentiate or Die

SPEED READING – ONE BRAND

Every company has a corporate brand.

But most are undifferentiated and uninspiring.

Here's the problem: People don't align with undifferentiated and uninspiring brands.

So, you must start by evaluating your corporate brand. (While your company may have many brands, it is your *corporate* brand that ultimately creates alignment.)

Your corporate brand has many functions.

First, your corporate brand must be an umbrella. It must be large enough to cover all your products and services. It must work in all your geographies. It must appeal to all your stakeholders.

While some will debate the "extendibility" of a corporate brand, Virgin uses theirs for *every* business they enter. Obviously, this creates alignment across their entire portfolio.

Second, your corporate brand must identify who you are and differentiate you from your competitors. Some of the key components of your corporate brand include:

- Your company name

- Your corporate logo

- Your corporate visual identity

- Your corporate value proposition

- Your corporate personality

- Your corporate tagline

So, perhaps you are thinking, "We have these things … so, we are aligned, right?"

Remember, people don't align with undifferentiated and uninspiring brands. So, just because you have them does not automatically mean that they are any good.

Finally, your corporate brand must be a powerful magnet. It must attract the right people—including employees, customers, partners, and investors—to your company.

In this chapter, we will explore how fast-lane companies like Virgin, UPS, the Government Employees Insurance Company, Chick-fil-A, and De Beers unleashed the accelerating power of alignment by creating a corporate brand so powerful that millions of people *want* to align with it.

VIRGIN

The Virgin Group (www.virgin.com) is a global conglomerate of over sixty businesses in five core sectors: Travel & Leisure, Telecoms & Media, Music & Entertainment, Financial Services, and Health & Wellness. Their portfolio companies employ 69,000 employees in 35 countries.

Virgin unleashed the accelerating power of alignment with One Brand.

In 1970, Richard Branson—now Sir Richard Branson—started a record company.

Recalling the origins of the Virgin brand name, Branson said: "I was 16 years old, sitting around with a bunch of girls, and I'd come up with the name Slipdisk Records for our new record company, and one of the girls said, 'No, call it Virgin. We're all virgins, you're a virgin in business.' So, we decided on Virgin, and then I couldn't get it registered in the registry office for four years because they thought the word Virgin was rude. In the end, I wrote a letter to them quoting the English dictionary to show it means pure, untouched, it's the opposite of rude. So finally, they gave it to me."

Virgin has become one of the most valuable brands in the world. It is also one of the most recognizable with 99 percent brand recognition in the UK and 96 percent in the U.S.

In addition to the unique logo and the color red, the brand creates alignment across the portfolio of businesses with six brand values: heartfelt service, delightfully surprising, red hot, straight up, insatiable curiosity, and smart disruption.

Lisa Thomas is the Managing Director and global head of brand at Virgin Enterprises. Here is how she described the process of managing the One Brand strategy, "Sometimes we lack focus and my job is to ensure we are brilliant and consistent where it matters. Not just around the brand, the logo—but also around our business mantra: happy people make happy customers, which makes for happy shareholders."

Many people think a brand is a logo.

In reality, it is much more than that. It expresses who you are, what you believe, why you exist, what you do, and more.

The Virgin brand permeates every molecule of the company. The brand is infused into the culture, the vision, the mission, the values, the colors, the tone of voice, the services, and even the architecture of the office space.

In addition, the Virgin brand extends into human resources, since people are "the personification of the brand."

Clearly, the One Brand strategy has produced amazing results. Virgin Records was the first Virgin company to reach a billion-dollar valuation in 1992. Since then, eight other Virgin-branded companies have become billion-dollar enterprises.

Does your company create alignment with a One Brand strategy?

UPS

UPS (NYSE: UPS) has 481,000 employees, 5,000 UPS Stores, 1,990 facilities, 123,000 delivery vehicles, 248 jet aircraft, and 316 chartered aircraft.

UPS unleashed the accelerating power of alignment with One Color.

UPS is enormous. But it all started with One Entrepreneur in One City with One Idea.

In 1907, James Casey founded the American Messenger Company in Seattle, Washington.

In 1919, the company expanded to serve the Oakland, California, market and changed its name to United Parcel Service. The change was to remind the company that operations were still *united*.

Even in 1919—One Century ago—alignment was critical to success!

The brown color used by UPS is called Pullman Brown. Legend has it that the brown color was chosen because it would make it easier to keep their trucks clean.

Amazingly, UPS has a trademark on its unique shade of brown.

Every company has a color palette. But only a few literally own One Color.

It seems like such a simple thing. Trivial, really.

There are thousands of books about corporate strategy and competitive advantage.

Yet UPS leveraged the simplest and humblest of colors to create an amazing competitive position.

Immediately recognizable. A global One-of-a-Kind.

For eight years, UPS ran an advertising campaign that asked, "What can brown do for you?"

Perhaps it is time to consider a different question, "What could owning One Color do for you?"

Just to be clear, there is a big difference between having a corporate color palette that your ad agency created and owning One Color.

Does your company have One Signature Color?

GOVERNMENT EMPLOYEES INSURANCE COMPANY

The Government Employees Insurance Company employs more than 40,000 associates in 17 major offices around the United States.

They unleashed the accelerating power of alignment with a clear and compelling value proposition.

Never heard of them? The Government Employees Insurance Company is commonly known as GEICO (www.geico.com).

"Fifteen minutes can save you fifteen percent or more on car insurance."

GEICO started running the "fifteen percent" campaign (developed by The Martin Agency in Richmond, Virginia) in 1999.

In 2013, they even added a parody campaign where someone reads a "fifteen percent" ad and a second person sarcastically says, "Everybody knows that."

Fifteen minutes.

Fifteen percent.

One message.

For over fifteen years.

Alignment is both an internal and an external issue. Creating a clear and memorable tagline creates brand alignment for GEICO with consumers. It also provides tremendous clarity to everyone inside the company.

Every decision can be evaluated based on its alignment with the brand promise.

GEICO has done such an amazing job owning their value proposition that every competitor has been forced to find a different one.

Clearly, the campaign has produced incredible results. Since launching the "fifteen percent" campaign, GEICO has grown revenue from $5.6 billion to over $26 billion!

Having One Tagline is a highly effective way of creating alignment. Assuming, that is, you have the discipline to stay with One.

Does your company have One clear and compelling value proposition?

CHICK-FIL-A

Chick-fil-A, Inc. (www.chick-fil-a.com) is a family-owned and privately held restaurant company founded in 1967 by S. Truett Cathy. Headquartered in Atlanta, Georgia, Chick-fil-A operates more than 2,300 restaurants in 47 states and Washington, D.C.

For more than 20 years, black-and-white Holstein cows have admonished us to "EAT MOR CHIKIN."

The rebel cows, as they are known, have painted their message of self-preservation on billboards, water towers, buildings, and more.

The real-life cows—including Kat, Freedom, Freckles, and Molly—have starred in dozens of television commercials and even have their own calendar—known as the Cowlendar.

In 2005, Chick-fil-A launched Cow Appreciation Day. Customers who come to a restaurant dressed as cows receive a free entrée. "Cow Appreciation Day is the one day where it's okay to dress 'udderly' crazy and get rewarded for it," quipped Jon Bridges, their Chief Marketing Officer.

The cows have even been inducted into New York's Madison Avenue Advertising Walk of Fame. (Coincidentally the campaign was also developed by The Martin Agency in Richmond, Virginia.)

The *EAT MOR CHIKIN* campaign has helped fuel the company's amazing growth. Twenty years ago, when Chick-fil-A started the campaign, they had 750 restaurants and less than $1B in revenue. Now they have over 2,300 restaurants and over $9B in revenue.

In addition, Chick-fil-A generates more revenue per store than any other fast food restaurant. The average Chick-fil-A unit generated around $4M in 2017. For comparison, the average McDonald's generated $2.7M and the average Starbucks generates $945K.

This is especially impressive since Chick-fil-A restaurants are closed on Sundays.

In addition to driving business results, the *EAT MOR CHIKIN* campaign provided a clear and consistent message that aligned the interests of franchisees, employees, and customers in a fun and engaging way.

The company credits much of its success to the stability of their leadership team. While corporate leaders at many quick-service restaurants change frequently, many senior leaders at Chick-fil-A have been with the company for more than 20 years.

They are also extremely selective when selecting their franchisees. Each year, over 40,000 people inquire about becoming a franchisee, but only about 100 get selected. Thus, becoming a Chick-fil-A franchisee is ten times harder than getting into Harvard!

"When we select someone, we select them for life," explained retired COO Jimmy Collins. Clearly, they apply that same thinking to advertising.

Does your company have One unique and endearing personality?

P.S. As it turns out, their frequent diner rewards program is called Chick-fil-A One™. They are speaking my language!

DE BEERS

GEICO has been using their slogan since 1999. Chick-fil-A has been using theirs since 1995.

But these pale in comparison to De Beers.

The De Beers Group (www.debeers.com), founded in 1888 by British businessman Cecil Rhodes, is a global powerhouse involved in multiple components of the diamond industry, including exploration, mining, retail, trading, and industrial diamond manufacturing.

In 1947, Frances Gerety, a young copywriter at the N. W. Ayer advertising agency in Philadelphia, created the slogan "A diamond is forever."

De Beers has been using it ever since. That's over seventy years!

The idea of engagement rings has been around since Medieval times. However, prior to this campaign, less than ten percent of engagement rings contained diamonds. The campaign was designed to create a situation where every person getting engaged felt compelled to give a ring with a diamond in it.

Their "A diamond is forever" campaign also set the benchmark for how much to spend—establishing the "two *months'* salary" rule that is still widely used today.

The campaign worked. Today, over 80 percent of women receive a diamond ring on their engagement.

From 1943 through 1970, Ms. Gerety wrote all the company's ads and was even featured in a novel called *The Engagements*, written by J. Courtney Sullivan.

"A diamond is forever" was recognized by Advertising Age as the greatest advertising slogan of the 20th century.

In 2008, De Beers leveraged their brand position to launch a new product line called Forevermark. Experts at the Forevermark Diamond Institute hand-pick the very best diamonds. (Of all the world's diamonds, less than one percent are eligible to become Forevermark.) Every Forevermark diamond is then inscribed with the Forevermark icon and a numerical code—invisible to the naked eye—that can forever identify the diamond and its authenticity.

At this point, I can hear the skeptics and contrarians questioning this strategy. After all, times change. Markets change. Consumers change. Products change.

Everything changes!

Yes, but a well-crafted message can indeed stand the test of time. Perhaps De Beers should say that "A tagline is forever."

If your advertising agency asked you to commit to One Tagline for seventy years, how would you respond?

SUMMARY – ONE BRAND

Your corporate brand impacts everything.

The best way to build One is to stand for something.

In this chapter, we explored how companies unleashed the accelerating power of alignment with great branding.

Virgin is—and always has been—cool. For nearly One Hundred years, UPS has been brown—Pullman Brown to be exact. GEICO saves you fifteen percent— everybody knows that. Chick-fil-A is udderly crazy. De Beers is forever.

Everyone is bombarded with thousands of messages every day. To break through, we recommend that you focus on One. Consistency is an essential component of creating a powerful corporate brand. The more frequently your message changes, the harder it is for people to align with it.

How about your company? Consider the following CHECKPOINTS to evaluate your corporate brand:

- Does your company have a unique and differentiating corporate brand?

- Does your company have a clear and compelling corporate brand promise?

- Does your company have an immediately recognizable corporate brand identity?

- Does your corporate communications campaign deliver One Message?

- How frequently does your message change?

ONE
STRATEGY

"Active Strategy Management enables companies to iterate, align, measure, and execute on strategic priorities faster and more transparently."

Deidre Paknad
Founder and CEO
Workboard, Inc.

SPEED READING – ONE STRATEGY

Every company has a corporate strategy.

But most people don't understand what it is.

In a Strategy& survey of more than 1,900 executives, an astounding 80 percent said their strategy was not well understood within their own company.

Obviously, people can't align with—or execute—a strategy they don't understand.

Strategy is "one of those words." Every company needs One, but even the strategy consulting firms don't have a common definition for what a strategy is.

Rather than create a new definition of strategy or propose yet another framework, this chapter focuses on five critical strategy questions every company must answer in order to provide clarity to the organization:

- Which market segment(s) should you target?

- What product(s) and/or service(s) should you sell?

- Where should you compete?

- How much should you charge?

- What is your business model?

To unleash the accelerating power of alignment, your company must answer them clearly and precisely.

Unfortunately, many companies struggle to do this. If they even have a strategy, it could be summarized as "more." More markets, more proposals, more products, more cities, etc.

The problem is that sometimes, more is less.

In contrast, fast-lane companies are much more disciplined about their strategy. In this chapter, we will look at how USAA, Basecamp, Iridium, Dollar Tree, and TOMS answered the five strategy questions.

Obviously, there are many other strategy questions that must be answered. Many of these are functional strategies. The Chief Financial Officer must develop a strategy to finance the company's operations. The Chief Marketing Officer must develop a strategy to build awareness and demand. The Chief People Officer must develop a strategy to recruit, retain, and develop the very best people. However, for the purposes of this section, we will focus on the five corporate strategy questions.

USAA

In 1922, 25 Army officers met in San Antonio, Texas, and decided to insure each other's vehicles. Today, the United Services Automobile Association—commonly known as USAA (www.usaa.com)—is a Fortune 500 financial services conglomerate offering banking, investing, and insurance to over 12 million people.

USAA unleashed the accelerating power of alignment with an intense focus on One Market.

Most companies want to sell their products and services to everyone. In contrast, USAA is focused on the unique needs of military families. In fact, membership is tightly restricted to four categories of people:

1. Currently Serving: Individuals who are currently serving in the U.S. Air Force, Army, Coast Guard, Marines, Navy, National Guard, and Reserves.

2. Former Military: Those who have retired or separated from the U.S. military with a discharge type of Honorable.

3. Family: Children, current spouses, widows, widowers, and unremarried former spouses of USAA members who had USAA auto or property insurance while married and individuals whose parents have or had USAA auto or property insurance.

4. Cadets or Midshipmen: Cadets and midshipmen at U.S. service academies, in advanced ROTC or on ROTC scholarship, plus officer candidates within 24 months of commissioning.

This narrow scope allows USAA to understand their customers better than their unfocused competitors. It also allows them to tailor their services to the unique needs of the military. In addition, a significant percentage of USAA's employees are former military members themselves.

"At USAA, we are passionate advocates for military members and their families. The same core values that guide our military inspire USAA employees to go above and beyond for our members each and every day."

This tight alignment has produced phenomenal results.

In October 2017, the Temkin Group released a research report ("Net Promoter Score Benchmark Study, 2017") based on a study of 10,000 U.S. consumers.

With a Net Promoter Score (NPS) of 66, USAA's insurance business earned the highest score in the study for the fifth year in a row.

In addition, USAA has long been widely recognized for being a great place to work including FORTUNE 100 Best Companies to Work For® and the Gallup Great Workplace Award.

Focusing on One Market unleashed the accelerating power of alignment for USAA. This strategy worked for them, and perhaps it is right for you.

After all, it is better to dominate One Market than dabble in dozens of them.

Is your company intensely focused on dominating One Market?

BASECAMP

Basecamp (www.basecamp.com) is a software company that developed a very successful project management application called Basecamp. After Basecamp, they developed a number of additional products including Backpack (an online information management tool), Campfire (an online chat service), and Highrise (a CRM application).

To improve strategic alignment, they pruned their portfolio to focus exclusively on just One Product.

In 2014, Basecamp became a "One Product" company solely focused on Basecamp. They even changed the name of the company from 37signals to Basecamp.

Instead of following the conventional wisdom about growth through diversification, they doubled down on Basecamp. This allowed the company to align their resources—human and financial—on becoming truly world-class at project management.

Here is how Jason Fried, co-founder of Basecamp, described the process, "We keep talking about doing more things, but we haven't entertained the other option: Do fewer. So, I want to pitch something radical. I want us to put all of our efforts into a single product—our main product, Basecamp."

Some might argue with the wisdom of putting "all of your eggs in One Basket," but the strategy has worked.

Since 2014, the user base of Basecamp has more than doubled.

The privately held company is highly regarded and was recognized by Forbes magazine as one of their "Small Giants 2017: America's Best Small Companies."

The more products and services your company offers, the harder it is to maintain alignment. When you have multiple product and service lines, resources can get diluted.

Having multiple products and services means multiple development teams. Multiple marketing teams. Multiple sales teams. Multiple pricing models. Multiple customer service and support teams.

In addition, customers naturally expect your multiple products and services to integrate. They want to get volume discounts. They want a consolidated contract.

All of these things create complexity. And the more complex your business becomes, the harder it is to align.

Focusing on One Product unleashed the accelerating power of alignment for Basecamp. This strategy worked for them and perhaps it is right for you.

After all, it is better to have One (Great) Product than dozens of mediocre ones.

Should you consider pruning your portfolio to focus on just One Product?

IRIDIUM

Iridium® Communications Inc. (NASDAQ: IRDM) is the only satellite communications company that offers truly global voice and data communications coverage.

Iridium creates strategic alignment by focusing on just One Planet.

I was surprised to learn that more than 80 percent of the Earth does not have cellular coverage. Iridium's strategy is to address that opportunity.

Iridium reinforces their global positioning with a One Word Tagline: Everywhere. And when your tagline is Everywhere, you must back it up.

In January 2019, the company completed their $3B Iridium NEXT project. Iridium NEXT is a network of 66 cross-linked Low-Earth Orbit (LEO) satellites, providing coverage over 100 percent of the earth's surface. Since these LEO satellites are "only" 476 miles from the Earth, Iridium's network has a shorter transmission path, stronger signals, and lower latency.

Iridium solutions are ideally suited for applications that demand global coverage. These include the maritime, aviation, government, military, emergency services, and more.

Matt Desch, Iridium's CEO, said, "Alignment is critical. Our customers know we differentiate by not making compromises on coverage. Even though we serve the whole planet, we only do what we do best. We don't try to be all things to all people but focus on the unique markets and customers where we have a distinct network advantage."

Deciding *where* to compete is one of the most important strategic decisions a company must make.

One way to create alignment is to compete in just One Geography. For your company, that might be one ZIP code or one city. This is an exceptional way to create alignment, since all your energy is intensely focused.

While Iridium was global from day one, most companies follow a more predictable pattern. They expand from local to regional to national to multinational and ultimately become truly global companies.

Clearly, the "One Planet" strategy has worked for Iridium. While their geographic footprint is global, they are intensely focused on their unique customer niche. Over the last decade, their revenues have more than doubled to over $500 million—and profitability has soared.

How do you define your geographic footprint?

DOLLAR TREE

Dollar Tree (NASDAQ: DLTR) has 14,300 stores, employs 180,000 people, and generates over $20 billion in revenue.

Dollar Tree unleashed the accelerating power of alignment by focusing on One Price Point.

This is an amazing story. Dollar Tree has built a $20+ billion-dollar company selling products for One Dollar!

Headquartered in Chesapeake, Virginia, Dollar Tree is the largest single-price-point retailer in North America. (Their late founder and CEO, Macon F. Brock Jr., wrote an autobiography about his experience. The title? *One Buck at a Time.*)

In 2015, the company acquired Family Dollar, solidifying their leadership in the single-price-point category. Of course, integrating—aka aligning—the two companies is a key priority. Some of their key initiatives include:

- Implementing a shared services model across corporate support functions, including Finance, Human Resources, Information Technology, and Supply Chain

- Introducing common technology platforms and processes across both brands

- Improving logistic and supply chain efficiencies

In November 2018, Gary Philbin, Dollar Tree's President and Chief Executive Officer, described their results, "Dollar Tree delivered its 43rd consecutive quarter of same-store sales growth, with increases in both customer transactions and average ticket. We are pleased with the performance of our newly renovated Family Dollar stores. Additionally, we have begun the important phase of consolidating our store support centers into our Chesapeake campus, which will improve our ability to support Family Dollar stores through enhanced collaboration, communication and teamwork."

Choosing a price point is an important component of your corporate strategy. Dollar Tree chose a very specific and easily understood One.

Of course, there are many different price points in every market.

On the low end, there is free. On the high end, there is IYHTAYCAI, which stands for "if you have to ask, you can't afford it."

The question for you to consider is whether your company should create strategic alignment by choosing One of them.

Your company can be Dollar Tree, or you can be Neiman Marcus. But not both.

Choosing One Price Point worked for Dollar Tree. In the last decade, their revenue has grown fivefold!

Where on the price point continuum does your company compete?

TOMS

TOMS® (www.toms.com) started as a simple shoe company, but has diversified into eyewear, coffee, and childbirth services.

They changed the world with their One for One® Business Model.

While vacationing in Argentina in 2006, TOMS founder Blake Mycoskie witnessed the hardships faced by children growing up without shoes. Wanting to help, he created TOMS Shoes, a company that would match every pair of shoes purchased with a new pair of shoes for a child in need.

TOMS calls their unique business model "One for One®."

Since its inception, TOMS has provided over 60 million pairs of shoes.

TOMS Eyewear launched in 2011 and has helped restore sight to over 400,000 people.

In 2014, TOMS expanded into coffee roasting and uses the proceeds to provide a one-week supply of water to a person in need.

At first glance, the business strategy would seem to violate the basic corporate strategy principle of focus.

After all, what do shoes, glasses, and coffee have in common?

All of TOMS' businesses operate with the same One for One business model. It is their inspiring raison d'être that keeps them aligned.

In 2014, TOMS sold a 50 percent equity stake in the company to Bain Capital. Private equity firms are generally not known for their social consciousness, but here is how Mycoskie described the deal:

> "We need a strategic partner who shares our bold vision for the future and can help us realize it. We're thrilled that Bain Capital is fully aligned with our commitment to One for One, and clearly they have the expertise to help us improve our business and further expand the scale of our mission."

In fact, the terms of the deal specified that the One for One approach would always be part of the TOMS business model.

Like TOMS, your company has a business model. For TOMS, their unique business model is 100 percent aligned with their unique purpose.

What is your company's business model?

NOTE: One for One® is a trademark of TOMS shoes.

SUMMARY – ONE STRATEGY

The worst strategy in the world is trying to be all things to all people.

In contrast, our exemplar companies are intensely focused.

USAA dominates One Market. Basecamp focuses on One Product. Iridium covers One Planet. Dollar Tree built a $20B company with One Price Point. TOMS unifies all of their ventures with the One for One business model.

Strategic alignment starts with having a great strategy. After all, smart people don't align with dumb strategies.

Perhaps your company's strategy is too broad or complex. If so, you may have to exit markets, prune products, shrink your footprint, or tighten your price point.

Assuming that you do indeed have a great strategy, then you must communicate it clearly and effectively. Of course, then you must align everyone—and everything—with it.

How about your company? Can you answer the five strategy questions clearly and precisely? Consider the following CHECKPOINTS:

- Who is your target customer?

- What product(s) and service(s) do you sell?

- Where do you compete?

- How much do you charge?

- What is your business model?

- Is everything synthesized and aligned as One Strategy?

"Aligned organizations achieve higher levels of performance because everyone is focused on driving measurable objectives. When you align teams, resources, planning, and processes, you reduce wasted time and misdirected efforts."

Zorian Rotenberg
Chief Executive Officer
Atiim

SPEED READING – ONE PORTFOLIO

Most companies sell multiple products and services.

But they often struggle to align them.

One way to create alignment is to literally sell just One Product. As we just learned, Basecamp chose this strategy.

However, most companies offer multiple products and services. Often, these are developed in different divisions. And divisions—by definition—divide.

In the 1970s, Bruce Henderson from the Boston Consulting Group introduced the concept of product portfolio management. His now famous "growth-share matrix" categorized a company's products as cash cows, stars, question marks, or dogs.

Perhaps your company still uses this management tool to manage your product portfolio.

Once you decide to develop multiple products, your business becomes more complex, and alignment becomes exponentially harder.

In some cases, customers may not have any expectations of product alignment. For example, people do not expect seamless interoperability between Proctor and Gamble's Tide, Pampers, and Crest products.

However, in most cases, customers will indeed expect some level of alignment. For example:

- They may expect your products to have a similar look and feel.

- They may expect your products to work together.

- They may expect your products to share common components.

This means you will have to develop corporate standards for product alignment and interoperability. These standards are an important component of your corporate core.

In this chapter, we will explore how BMW, LEGO, RYOBI and HubSpot aligned their product portfolio to create both synergies and differentiation.

BMW

In 1933, a fledgling company known as Bayerische Motoren Werke GmbH (DE: BMW) introduced the BMW 303.

It was the first BMW to use the now iconic kidney grille.

For eighty-five years, the kidney grille has been used on all BMW cars with just four exceptions (the 937–1940 BMW 325, the 1955–1962 BMW Isetta, the 1957–1959 BMW 600, and the 1959–1962 BMW 700).

Although the function of the kidney grille was to help cool down the engine, BMW even used it on the electric i3 and the hybrid i8.

The kidney grille is BMW's signature design element. It provides a unifying—and immediately recognizable—visual identity for all their products. It unifies their dozens of models into One Portfolio.

Having the management discipline to stay with this One Style for eighty-five years is an impressive feat. I'm sure that many BMW designers have complained that having to use the kidney grille on every car was hindering their creativity.

In fact, the original design for the first e21 3-series BMW (produced from 1975–1983) ditched the kidney design in favor of a more GM-like grille with horizontal bars. Thankfully, Bob Lutz, who was executive vice president of sales at BMW North America, convinced the company to redesign the car with the kidney grille.

I believe the decision to stay with the design standard has been an important component of BMW's success and growth. In 1974, BMW was the 11th largest European brand in the U.S., selling just over 15,000 cars. Now, they sell over 300,000 cars per year.

In my book, *Decide One Thing*, I also profiled BMW.

In 1975, BMW unveiled "The Ultimate Driving Machine" tagline. (Interestingly, the tagline was also created by Bob Lutz.)

They had the discipline to stay with One Tagline for thirty-five years! But in 2010, they abandoned The Ultimate Driving Machine for the much maligned "Joy" campaign.

In 2012, they brought back The Ultimate Driving Machine. In fact, the ad copy was, "We don't make sports cars. We don't make SUVs. We don't make hybrids. We don't make luxury sedans. We only make One Thing: The Ultimate Driving Machine." (That's why this story was a perfect fit for my *Decide One Thing* book!)

Then, they switched again and started using "Sheer Driving Pleasure." In 2013, they started using another new slogan, "Designed for Driving Pleasure." A review of their websites for various countries around the world revealed that multiple taglines are used, including "The Ultimate Driving Machine."

Having a single, unifying product design element can be a powerful way to create alignment. For 85 years, BMW has had the discipline to stay with it. I just wish they had the same discipline with their tagline.

Do your products and/or services have One single, unifying design element?

LEGO

LEGO® (www.lego.com) was founded in 1932 by Ole Kirk Kristiansen. The privately held, family-owned company with headquarters in Billund, Denmark, has over 19,000 employees and operates 132 LEGO brand stores.

They have built an amazing business, One Brick at a time.

My mom recently spent time cleaning and sorting the LEGO bricks my brothers and I played with as kids so she could donate them to a local church. These bricks are almost 60 years old and they are still viable. In fact, all LEGO bricks produced since 1958 are fully compatible with the bricks produced today.

Every year, LEGO sells over 75 billion bricks and other components that they call "elements." There are more than 3,700 different types of pieces, including bricks, wheels, motors, swords, figures, and more.

These are manufactured with incredible precision—the molds used to produce LEGO elements are accurate to within 0.004 mm—less than the width of a single hair. This accuracy ensures that the bricks will have what LEGO calls "clutch power."

Since LEGO's mission is to "inspire and develop the builders of tomorrow," they often take on special projects to demonstrate the amazing things that can be built with LEGOs.

In 2018, they built a full-scale copy of the $3M Bugatti Chiron sports car out of LEGO bricks! It took over 13,000 man-hours to build and used over 1 million LEGO elements. It has 2,304 LEGO motors and a top speed of 12 MPH (versus 261 MPH for the real one!) The Bugatti factory test driver and multiple Le Mans champion Andy Wallace had the honor of the first drive.

The LEGO Chiron is truly amazing. But let's just say you only have *six* two-by-four bricks. There are 915,103,765 ways to combine them! I spent hours as a kid building things, breaking them down, and then using my imagination to build something else.

LEGO is an amazing example of how a standardized product architecture can create alignment. There are a number of key insights that companies should consider applying.

First is backward compatibility. LEGO bricks that were built sixty years ago still interoperate with the current ones.

The second key insight is the power of modularity. People can mix and match LEGO elements to build virtually anything. Many companies struggle to create cross-divisional product portfolios. Creating a common architecture can ensure that products from division 1 interoperate with products from division 2.

It worked for LEGO. The company is worth over $7 billion, making it the world's most valuable toy brand by far, according to consultancy Brand Finance.

Does your company have One unifying product architecture that keeps everything aligned?

RYOBI

In 1996, RYOBI introduced a cordless drill with an 18V battery system called ONE+.

Now, they sell an integrated portfolio of ONE+ compatible products.

Ryobi Technologies, Inc., is an Anderson, South Carolina-based subsidiary of Techtronic Industries Co. Ltd. (SEHK: 669).

The RYOBI 18V ONE+ System features over 125 unique products, including drills, saws, vacuums, mowers, blowers, trimmers, nailers, grinders, augers, and even floating Bluetooth speakers for your pool.

One component of the RYOBI brand promise is that they will *never* change the 18V ONE+ battery platform. That means that their newest products and batteries fit the original RYOBI tools and batteries from 1996.

They have used the same system for over twenty years!

The RYOBI ONE+ strategy is a great example of how alignment can start with One Product and expand into a portfolio of fully compatible products.

When a company pledges to *never* change their system, consumers can buy with confidence.

Their pledge also provides a tremendous differentiator. Once you buy your first RYOBI ONE+ product, the next time you go shopping for tools, RYOBI will be your preferred vendor.

You'll head over to Home Depot (RYOBI tools and batteries are available exclusively at The Home Depot) and look for their distinctive "hyper green" color. (Yes, all their tools also feature One Color, further reinforcing their integration as One Portfolio.)

When you compare tools, the RYOBI will be the cheapest alternative, since you can buy the new tools without the battery.

I spent most of my career in the technology business. Unfortunately, the technology industry has refused to learn this lesson.

I have a drawer full of obsolete Apple power cords, cables, dongles, and other stuff. Entire landfills have been consumed with Apple's e-trash alone.

Imagine if Apple had promised consumers that they would *never* change their iPhone power cord? Imagine if the same power cord worked on your iPhone, your iPod, your iPad, and your MacBook.

Does your company have One component that will never change?

HUBSPOT

In 2004, Brian Halligan and Dharmesh Shah met as graduate students at the Massachusetts Institute of Technology (MIT). Two years later, they started HubSpot (NYSE: HUBS). The company now has over 52,000 customers (including SHIFTPOINTS) in more than 100 countries.

HubSpot built an impressive ecosystem of add-on products.

The company started as a software-as-a-service (SAAS) application for marketing. They evolved into an integrated suite that includes customer relationship management (CRM), sales, service, and more.

While only a few vendors offer what HubSpot calls the full "growth stack," most customers require specialized add-on products to achieve their goals.

Choosing the right add-on products is a mind-numbing task. This segment of the software market is massively crowded. In fact, there are over 6,000 software vendors building specialized marketing, sales, and service products.

In addition, most customers require integrations between HubSpot and their other applications.

To address the problem, HubSpot developed an ecosystem called HubSpot Connect. It includes a portfolio of certified add-on products and application programming interfaces (APIs).

As a result, HubSpot now describes themselves as a "platform company." They already boast over 200 software integrations with several new partners joining each month.

The HubSpot ecosystem expands the functionality of HubSpot's core product offerings and helps customers find the add-on solutions that are right for their business.

"Our platform partners offer customers an incredible range of specialized capabilities they can easily add to HubSpot," said Scott Brinker, HubSpot's VP of platform ecosystem. "Together, we strive to make it a seamless experience."

"We're laser-focused on scaling the HubSpot Connect partner program to give our customers all of the tools they need to grow their business," said Brad Coffey, Chief Strategy Officer at HubSpot.

Does your company have One Ecosystem of partners that adds value to your core offering?

SUMMARY – ONE PORTFOLIO

One of the best growth strategies is to increase your "share of wallet."

Aligning your product(s) and service(s) into One Portfolio can help you do it.

BMW unified their portfolio with a kidney grille. LEGO's modular architecture unified the portfolio, one brick at a time. RYOBI has pledged to *never* change their ONE+ battery platform. HubSpot connected an ecosystem of compatible software applications.

How about your company? Which strategy do you use?

Consider the following CHECKPOINTS to evaluate your product portfolio:

- Does your company have a signature design element?

- Does your company have a unifying product architecture?

- Are your products backward—and forward—compatible?

- Is there one component of your product design that will never change?

- What percentage of your customers have bought your entire portfolio?

"There are two roadblocks. One is that the CEO does not take the time to communicate a sense of urgency throughout the organization about the need to change. The second is that the organization does not realign all the processes within the institution with the strategic imperatives."

Louis Gerstner
Former CEO
IBM

SPEED READING – ONE WAY

Every company has corporate standards.

But most have never optimized them.

When something is a corporate standard, it means that you have One—and Only One—Way of doing something. This might be as mundane as having One—and Only One—Way to complete an expense form or as significant as having One—and Only One—Way to perform heart transplants.

Companies make all kinds of things a corporate standard, such as:

- Their unique way of doing business

- Mission-critical business processes

- Policies or rules

- Dress codes

- Software applications

- The exact size and furniture for every office

- And more

Theoretically, these corporate standards are absolutely, positively, and nonnegotiably the same everywhere in your company.

Everyone must comply with them. No exceptions.

For nearly 16 years, Jenny Wu, an amazing stylist at Bubbles Hair Salon in Reston, Virginia, has cut my hair. Part of Bubbles' One Way is a dress code: stylists are *required* to wear black. If a stylist shows up with purple hair, they get commended. It they show up in a purple shirt, they get sent home to change clothes.

While standardization can improve alignment, we advise companies to find the right balance. If nothing is standardized, there is chaos and anarchy. If everything is standardized, your company is a stifling bureaucracy.

We learned of an insurance brokerage that required every employee to write in blue ink. That sounds pretty stifling.

In contrast, UPS trains their drivers to "always" turn right. This standard was based on extensive analysis of traffic and route efficiency. That sounds smart—and the corporate standard was fully embraced.

In this chapter, we will explore how Bognet Construction, Formula One, Starbucks, and ING unleashed the accelerating power of alignment by standardizing their One Way.

BOGNET CONSTRUCTION

Bognet Construction (www.bognet.com) is a rapidly growing commercial general contractor in Washington, D.C.

They unleashed the accelerating power of alignment with The BOGNET Way.

"The BOGNET Way transformed our company," said Jennifer Bognet, "It captures the essence of who we are, how we work, and why customers should choose us."

In 2008, the company went through a process to codify their unique business philosophy. This led to the creation of The BOGNET Way, and the results have been very impressive.

First, it allowed Bognet to differentiate their company from their competitors. After all, many general contractors can manage construction, but only One Company does it The BOGNET Way.

Second, it allowed Bognet to optimize their human capital. From recruiting to training to recognition, The BOGNET Way provides accelerating clarity. They use The BOGNET Way to evaluate applicants. They also use The BOGNET Way as their framework for employee recognition.

Below are the six components of The BOGNET Way:

> **B**UILD LONG-TERM RELATIONSHIPS
> We strive to build long-term relationships with every member of the project team. Because we are focused on the long-term, these relationships are a critical element of how we work, how we solve problems, and how we communicate.

> **O**PERATE AS ONE TEAM
> We work to provide strong leadership to all parties in the job (architect, tenant, construction manager, building owner, subcontractors, etc.) with the goal of working together as one integrated team.

GO THE EXTRA MILE
We are relentless about the details of every project and aggressively follow-up until the job is done. Before every employee leaves for the day, they ask themselves, "Have I done everything possible to anticipate tomorrow's problems today?"

NEVER STOP IMPROVING
We are committed to look for innovative new ways to deliver our projects, applying the latest tools and procedures to improve efficiency. We work hard to stay on top of industry trends and innovations.

ENGINEER WIN-WIN SOLUTIONS
We strive to balance the needs of all parties in the project to find the win-win solution. We look for creative ways to solve challenges, and resolve conflicts so we can deliver exceptional quality.

TAKE OWNERSHIP
At Bognet, we will do whatever it takes to deliver on our promises. The Bognet Executive Team is highly engaged in every project as an executive sponsor.

As you can see, it is an acrostic, which makes it easy for everyone to remember. Even better, it provides a structured way for Bognet to deliver exceptional construction projects for their clients.

Since implementing The BOGNET Way, the company has *quintupled* in size.

Has your company codified your unique way of doing business?

FORMULA ONE

The FIA Formula One World Championship
(www.formula1.com) is the premier global racing league,
with ten teams, twenty drivers, and twenty races worldwide.

This fast-moving sport is governed by One Formula.

Formula One cars are the fastest road course racing cars in
the world. (Juan Pablo Montoya owns the record for the
fastest top speed—231.523 mph—recorded during the 2005
Italian Grand Prix.)

In addition, Formula One racing is a big business.

In 2017, Formula One generated profits of around $1.8
billion. One half is divided among the Formula One teams in
a complex profit-sharing formula, and the other half goes to
the Formula One group and shareholders.

The sport is governed by the Fédération Internationale de
l'Automobile (FIA), which publishes and enforces the rules
of the sport. These rules are known as "the formula," hence
the name of the series.

These detailed regulations govern all aspects of the sport,
down to the smallest detail.

The FIA Sporting Regulations document is over 70 pages
long and covers things like the points system, the size of
logos on the cars, and even the length of the press
conference.

The FIA Technical Regulations document is over 100 pages
long and provides specific rules and regulations for every
aspect of the car, from the exact height of the rear wing, the
number of forward gears, and even the exact materials that
wheels must be constructed from.

These regulations are strictly enforced, and FIA stewards have the power to impose penalties on a driver and/or team for violating them.

Every company has rules and regulations. As we explained, some have too few, but most have too many.

Formula One creates strategic alignment by requiring every team to abide by One Formula, comprised of over 170 pages of rules and regulations. While that might sound ominous, it is what is required to keep the teams and drivers aligned.

Does your company have too many rules ... or too few?

STARBUCKS

Starbucks (NASDAQ: SBUX) has 254,000 employees working in 24,000 retail stores in 70 countries.

Although there are roughly 100,000 permutations of drinks, there is only One Way to make each One.

Coffee has always been my favorite beverage. So, when Starbucks barged on the scene in the early '90s, I was an early adopter. I have lost count of how many Starbucks I have visited in my life. Countless portions of this book have been written in Starbucks coffee shops around the world.

In the beginning, we all had to learn how to "speak Starbucks." Does "decaf" come before or after "grande"? Is it "two-pump no whip" or "no whip two pump?" What's the difference between a cappuccino and a Frappuccino®?

Some people never became fluent in Starbucks and are embarrassed to go there.

Most people, however, have developed a basic level of Starbucks ordering competence.

As I am sure you have experienced, they also have a very specific process to ensure that your order is properly communicated to the barista. It is called the "Starbucks® Beverage Calling & Cup Marking System," and even specifies that a *black* permanent marker be used to write beverage identification codes on cups.

And of course, they had to teach all their baristas how to make all those drinks.

My sense is that being a Starbucks barista is a lot harder than most people think. They must memorize the Starbucks beverage manual, which contains the exact specifications for every drink. And these specifications are extremely specific.

Did you know:

- Beverage temperature is between 150°F and 170°F not including Americanos. (Unless you order it extra hot.)

- An espresso shot should be 15–19 seconds for Verismo and 18–23 seconds for La San Marco.

- Blended beverages should be poured into the cup within 10 seconds of blending.

All of this is designed to fulfill The Starbucks Promise: "Your drink should be perfect, every time. If not, let us know and we'll make it right."

In order for Starbucks to fulfill their mission and deliver on their brand promise, they had to develop strict corporate standards.

There is only One Way to make a double-tall skim latte—my go-to drink.

Does your company have specific process standards for every product?

ING

The ING Group (ADRs: ING US, ING.N) is a Dutch multinational banking and financial services corporation headquartered in Amsterdam. (ING is an abbreviation for Internationale Nederlanden Groep.) They have more than 52,000 employees servicing customers in over 40 countries.

In 2015, they embraced the Agile Methodology as the ING Way.

ING began using Agile in 2010 with three software development teams. In 2011, they transitioned the entire development organization to Agile. Then, in 2015, ING decided to implement it for every part of their business. They call this, "The ING Way of Working" and they were the first bank to go all-in on Agile.

ING chose to embrace the Agile Methodology for three reasons:

- To be more efficient and more flexible

- To innovate faster with shorter time to market

- To be a more attractive employer

Here is how they describe their new organization:

> In the Agile Method, everyone works in squads: self-managing, autonomous units with end-to-end responsibility for a specific customer-focused project. A squad brings together colleagues from all the disciplines that are needed to complete the project successfully. At the end of the project, the squad is disbanded, and the members set to work in other squads. A squad works together in a shared space. To facilitate that and to offer inspiring work spaces, the ING head office in Amsterdam has been entirely revamped and so too has our office in Leeuwarden. No one at ING in the Netherlands has

their own office anymore—not even members of the board.

The squads form part of a bigger entity that operates along similar lines. Squads that are involved in the same area of work are part of an overarching tribe.

In principle, all activities are organized in squads, but we have created Centers of Expertise for scarce or specialized knowledge.

Most companies have rigidly delineated departments and divisions. ING has Agile squads and tribes.

This move might seem radical, but it feels aligned with their corporate purpose which is to "Empower people to stay a step ahead in life and in business."

Speaking of alignment, ING utilizes quarterly business reviews (QBRs) to keep the squads and tribes aligned with corporate priorities. They manage their transformation, which they call "Think Forward," from the Obeya room in Amsterdam. ("Obeya" is a Japanese term that roughly translates as "war room.")

The ING Way of Working started with three teams but has now transformed the entire company.

Does your company have One "way of working"?

SUMMARY – ONE WAY

Corporate standards are an essential component of alignment.

If you want your employees to drive in One Direction, you must show them the way.

Some companies have too many standards. Some have too few. Some have standards that are codified. Most also have many standards that are implied.

In this chapter, we explored how four fast-lane companies leveraged their One Way to accelerate alignment.

Bognet has quintupled since implementing The BOGNET Way. Every Formula One team must abide by "the formula." Every Starbucks barista knows the exact specifications for every one of the 100,000 permutations. ING went all-in on Agile.

How about your company? Consider the following CHECKPOINTS to evaluate your company's One Way:

- Have you identified, optimized, and institutionalized your mission-critical processes?

- What are your corporate rules and policies that everyone must align with?

- Does your company have too many corporate standards—or too few?

- Is your One Way internally or externally focused?

- How do you ensure that everyone is absolutely, positively, and nonnegotiably following your One Way?

"Every person in your company is a vector. Your progress is determined by the sum of all vectors."

Elon Musk
Chief Executive Officer
Tesla Motors

SPEED READING – ONE WOW!

Every company delivers a customer experience.

But most don't deliver One that makes customers say "Wow!"

Bain & Company analysis shows that "companies that excel in the customer experience grow revenues 4%–8% above their market. That's because a superior experience helps to earn stronger loyalty among customers, turning them into promoters who tend to buy more, stay longer, and make recommendations to their friends."

Your company is already delivering some type of customer experience.

The question, however, is whether you are delivering a *standardized* experience that makes customers say "Wow!"

Obviously, your company has many customers. Each customer is unique and expects a customer experience that is custom-fit to their unique needs and wants.

However, fast-lane companies also standardize foundational elements of their customer experience. Thus, their unique Wow! is both standardized and customized.

To start the standardization process, identify One Experience that will appeal to all your customers. For example, you could ensure that every employee always calls every customer by name.

Over time, you can design a more robust customer experience that is a blend of multiple elements.

Of course, you can't just develop a unique customer experience … you must deliver it.

Unfortunately, according to Gallup, only 27 percent of employees feel that their company always delivers what they promise.

Therefore, your company must develop the systems, processes, and culture to align everyone—and everything—to deliver your One Wow! … not one time but every time.

In this chapter, we will explore how The Ritz-Carlton, Costco, CrossFit, and Four Sisters unleashed the accelerating power of alignment by developing—and delivering—a standardized customer experience.

RITZ-CARLTON

The Ritz-Carlton (NASDAQ: MAR)* operates 91 hotels worldwide in 30 countries and territories. Their 40,000 employees are known as "the Ladies and Gentlemen of The Ritz-Carlton."

They set the gold standard for hospitality.

In fact, The Ritz-Carlton (yes, the "The" is always capitalized) actually calls their service delivery system The Gold Standard. It includes The Credo, a Motto, Three Steps of Service, Twelve Service Values, The Sixth Diamond, and an Employee Promise.

While many companies have these kinds of things, The Ritz-Carlton takes them the extra mile.

Herve Humler, their President and Chief Operating Officer, explained it this way, "Have a clear, compelling, and ambitious vision. Make sure people understand the vision, talk about it daily, and live it always. If you don't inscribe these things, they will go away."

They reinforce this every morning. Each day, The Ritz-Carlton hotels around the world participate in a Daily Line-Up. All employees—from front-line staff to the Chief Operating Officer—participate in this daily meeting. This gathering aligns employees with The Ritz-Carlton culture. During this meeting, they share "Wow" stories (yes, they actually call them Wow stories) about an employee who went above and beyond to deliver a unique service experience.

In addition, all the Ladies and Gentlemen around the globe participate in the annual SWOT (Strengths, Weaknesses, Opportunities, and Threats) analysis. By including *everyone* in this process, The Ritz-Carlton is demonstrating that every employee's ideas are valued.

Financial information such as budgets and revenue are shared with everyone at The Ritz-Carlton. Ladies and Gentlemen are aware of financial goals and openly discuss numbers. Not only does this instill accountability, but it also fosters a sense of ownership.

While every guest is unique and has unique needs, The Ritz-Carlton's Three Steps of Service explains how to deliver their unique Wow!:

1. A warm and sincere greeting.

2. Use the guest's name. Anticipation and fulfillment of each guest's needs.

3. Fond farewell. Give a warm good-bye and use the guest's name.

Part of their unique formula is to empower people to go the extra mile without asking permission from their manager. In fact, every employee can spend up to $2,000 to satisfy a guest.

While The Ritz-Carlton's service delivery philosophy is standardized, their hotel architecture is not. "We do not work to one design mold, but rather allow the process to be destination and customer focused." Each Ritz-Carlton property around the world has a unique design reflecting its location.

Does your company empower employees to do whatever is necessary to Wow! customers?

* The Ritz-Carlton is part of Marriott.

COSTCO

Costco Wholesale (NASDAQ: COST) is the second-largest retailer in the country with over $138 billion in sales. They have 243,000 employees, 773 warehouses in 10 countries, and 97 million members.

While no one will confuse Costco with The Ritz-Carlton, they also deliver an amazing Wow!

Costco's customer experience starts with their membership model, which creates an amazing alignment of interests. Once you pay your annual fee, you have an incentive to maximize the value of your membership by spending more at Costco. Thus, both customers and Costco have exactly the same goal—to maximize sales!

The revenue from membership fees is almost pure profit, and it typically makes up nearly 100 percent of Costco's net income. With this high-profit annuity as the baseline, Costco prices merchandise to just barely cover costs. Thus, customers know that when they see something at Costco, it is likely the best deal in town.

As a result, Costco has membership renewal rates above 90 percent!

Costco carries a wide selection of merchandise categories—everything from televisions to tires. But within those categories, a shopper's options are limited: the typical warehouse is stocked with fewer than 4,000 products, compared to 45,000 at a typical grocery store.

Costco is also the largest wine retailer in the U.S. While most wine retailers stock thousands of wines, a typical Costco store has only about 100. Most are low priced, but occasionally they will have very expensive bottles of French Bordeaux.

Shopping at Costco is a unique experience. To enter the warehouse, you must show your membership card. In a strange way, this creates a feeling of being part of an exclusive club—comprised of the world's savviest shoppers.

Because shoppers know that everything at Costco is "a great deal," it is very easy to buy things that were not on their shopping list. Customers come for a toaster and leave with a 72–inch high-definition television that was just too good to pass up. Most will enjoy the amazing selection of free samples or one of Costco's legendary $1.50 hot dog meals.

The warehouses are austere. No plush carpeting here. No fancy displays. Just concrete floors and metal warehouse shelving. Most of the merchandise is packaged in bulk, making it easy to buy a year's supply of toilet paper.

While Costco does not call their employees "Ladies and Gentlemen," they are always a big part of the customer experience. Costco has incredibly low turnover for a retailer—less than 1 percent for managers and less than 5 percent for hourly employees.

Over 75 percent of Costco warehouse managers started out as hourly employees, and their CEO, Craig Jelinek, started as a warehouse manager.

Costco proves that you don't have to be expensive to deliver an amazing Wow!

The company went public on December 5, 1985, at $10.00 per share. If you had bought shares at their IPO, you would have a return of 13,447 percent.

Wow!

How does your business model impact your customer experience?

CROSSFIT®

CrossFit (www.crossfit.com) has a global network of over 13,000 gyms known as affiliates. Their Facebook page has over 2.2 million followers. In addition to affiliates, there are CrossFit Games, CrossFit clothes, and a portfolio of accessories.

CrossFit unleashed the accelerating power of alignment with One Workout.

CrossFit is a fitness regimen developed by Greg Glassman. It is designed to optimize physical competence in ten fitness domains: cardiovascular and respiratory endurance, stamina, strength, flexibility, power, speed, coordination, agility, balance, and accuracy.

The Workout of the Day (WOD) is a key component of the CrossFit model. They describe their exercise philosophy this way:

> CrossFit is constantly varied functional movements performed at high intensity.
>
> All CrossFit workouts are based on functional movements, and these movements reflect the best aspects of gymnastics, weightlifting, running, rowing and more.
>
> While CrossFit challenges the world's fittest, the program is designed for universal scalability, making it the perfect application for any committed individual, regardless of experience. We scale load and intensity; we don't change the program. The needs of Olympic athletes and our grandparents differ by degree, not kind.

CrossFit gyms—affectionately known as "boxes" for their austere warehouse environment—are independent affiliates, not franchises. The affiliate licenses the CrossFit brand, but operates very independently.

Interestingly, while CrossFit "headquarters" publishes a new Workout of the Day every day, the affiliate gyms are free to use it or to develop their own.

In fact, a quick scan of the CrossFit affiliate gyms near my house revealed that *none* of them was using the WOD recommended by CrossFit headquarters for that day. Each affiliate had developed its own WOD.

While the specific exercises were different, the essence of the CrossFit WOD experience was maintained. Thus, CrossFit created an ecosystem of affiliates that are aligned in spirit.

This is an interesting approach to alignment. The corporate standard is really just a corporate suggestion, but it works for them. The CrossFit model of creating alignment in their ecosystem is aligned with their business strategy and corporate culture.

Alignment is always a balancing act between standardization and flexibility. CrossFit found the balance that works for them and their affiliates.

How does your company align your ecosystem to deliver your Wow!?

FOUR SISTERS

There are millions of restaurants in the world.

Four Sisters is—by far—my favorite One!

Four Sisters (http://www.foursistersrestaurant.com) is an award-winning Vietnamese restaurant in Falls Church, Virginia.

Originally from Bien Hoa, Vietnam, Kim Lai, his wife, Thanh Tran, their four daughters, Ly, Le, Lo Ann, and Lieu, and two sons, Hoa and Thuan, immigrated to the U.S. in 1982. Although Kim was a successful entrepreneur in Vietnam, the family came to America with nothing and essentially had to start over.

Kim started working in a food truck that sold hot dogs and other items to tourists in Washington, D.C. Eventually, he was able to buy his own food truck and grew the business to eight trucks.

In 1993, the family opened their first restaurant, a tiny place in the back corner of the Eden Center, an international shopping center in Falls Church, Virginia. It was called Huong Que, roughly translated as "taste of home."

Driven by Kim's entrepreneurial spirit and Thanh Tran's cooking, the restaurant quickly built a loyal following. In 1996, they were able to move to a larger space in a better location in the Eden Center. The four sisters—who are all strikingly beautiful—worked as hostesses and waitresses, and the restaurant started to be known as both Huong Que and Four Sisters.

They moved to their current location in the Merrifield Town Center in 2007. The family used the move to formally rebrand the restaurant as Four Sisters. They also saw it as an opportunity to design a unique customer experience.

Four Sisters blends four unique elements to create their unique Wow!

The first thing you notice upon entering the restaurant is the amazing flower arrangements. Le, the second-oldest sister, creates these herself. The multiple arrangements each consist of hundreds of flowers. She changes them every Thursday, so every visit provides a unique surprise.

"I can't cook," Le confessed, "but I am passionate about flowers. It is a labor of love."

Next, you will notice the amazing artwork. Le commissioned the paintings in Vietnam, and they took over six months to make.

Another aspect of the Four Sisters Wow! is the staff. While most restaurants experience tremendous turnover, many of the staff have been with the restaurant for decades. A few have been with them since the beginning. "We are like a big, extended family," explained Le.

And last—but certainly not least—is the delicious food. The menu is extensive—there are 152 unique dishes—including traditional Vietnamese favorites and French-inspired specialties such as Sup Mang Cua (crabmeat and asparagus soup).

In the beginning, Thanh Tran made everything herself, largely by feel. As the restaurant grew, they had to codify the recipes so that other chefs could deliver each dish perfectly every night.

I have been to hundreds of Vietnamese restaurants, but there is nothing like Four Sisters. For over two decades, they have delivered their unique, One-of-a-Kind experience with amazing consistency. This is why they have thousands of fans—like me—who eat there as often as possible.

Does your customer experience differentiate your company from everyone else?

SUMMARY – ONE WOW!

Developing a standardized customer experience is a great way to improve alignment.

Delivering it <u>every time</u> will make your customers say "Wow!"

The Ritz-Carlton's "Ladies and Gentlemen" deliver the gold standard. Costco's austere warehouses deliver an entirely different Wow! CrossFit's affiliates deliver a "Wow! That $#%*!# hurts—no pain, no gain" workout experience.

For nearly three decades, Four Sisters has delivered a unique—and astonishingly consistent—dining experience. I strongly recommend the Cha Gio and Bo Luc Lac. Wow! Yum! Tell Le Lai I sent you.

How about your company? Consider the following CHECKPOINTS to evaluate your company's One Wow!:

- Does your company have a unique and unifying corporate Wow!?

- How do you ensure that you deliver it every time?

- Are your people empowered to do whatever it takes to Wow! a customer?

- Are your customers raving fans?

- How many of your customers have written endorsements of the Wow! experience you deliver?

PLAN

"I've always thought that the biggest secret of Salesforce is how we've achieved a high level of organizational alignment and communication while growing at breakneck speeds."

Marc Benioff
Chairman and Co-CEO
Salesforce

SPEED READING – ONE PLAN

Every company makes plans.

For some, their long-range strategic plan outlines what they are going to do after lunch.

Fast-lane companies use both the planning process and the codified plan to accelerate alignment.

Unfortunately, according to Bain and Company, only 60 percent of executives think that their company's planning process is effective.

Ideally, the output of an effective planning process is One clearly codified Plan. Most corporate plans contain the following elements:

- A strategic plan

- An annual operating plan

- A financial forecast and associated departmental budgets

- A headcount plan

- Strategic initiatives (the critical few) that are essential to accomplishing the plan

Ideally, your company will have just One Plan.

To document the plan, some companies create a deck of slides, some create a narrative, some create infographics, and others use cloud-based software.

Our preference is to summarize it on One Page.

Regardless of how you document it, it is imperative that you effectively communicate it.

Obviously, people cannot execute a plan they don't understand.

In this chapter, we will explore the planning processes that Google, Salesforce, IDEXX, and Hagerty used to unleash the accelerating power of alignment.

GOOGLE

Google (NASDAQ: GOOG) has a huge mission: organize the world's information and make it universally accessible and useful.

They keep everyone—and everything—aligned with a system known as "OKRs."

The "Objectives and Key Results" model was developed by Andy Grove at Intel.

John Doerr, the chair of venture capital firm Kleiner Perkins, introduced the OKR system to Google in 1999, shortly after investing in the company. He describes OKRs as "a management methodology that helps to ensure that the company focuses efforts on the same important issues throughout the organization."

The first step in the process is to develop objectives. Objectives are sometimes described as "strategic themes" or "burning imperatives." Companies generally set no more than five corporate objectives. They should be clear, ambitious, and inspirational. For example, one of your objectives might be to "Develop a world-class workforce."

The next step is to develop a set of key results for each objective. These are specific, measurable, and much more tactical. Most companies will have three to five key results for each objective. For example, you might set a key result to "increase employee engagement from 75 percent to 85 percent."

These are company-wide OKRs, but for greater alignment, OKRs are often used at all levels. This helps ensure that all work is aligned with your goals.

There are a few aspects of Google's OKR model that differentiate them from other management systems.

"At our scale, it's important to focus and do it well," Sundar Pichai, CEO of Google, explained, "When you can align people to common goals, you truly get a multiplicative effect in an organization."

First, OKRs are based on transparency. Everyone can see everyone else's OKRs.

Second, at Google, OKRs are reset quarterly. They have done this since the beginning. Thus, for over seventy-five consecutive quarters, Google executives have thoughtfully and deliberately worked through the goal-setting and alignment process.

Third, Google separates the OKR process from the HR performance appraisal process. That is because they want the company—and every employee—to set extremely ambitious "moonshot" objectives.

In the nearly twenty years since Doerr introduced OKRs, Google has grown to over 80,000 employees. And OKRs have been a key component of their success.

"OKRs have helped lead us to 10X growth, many times over." said Alphabet CEO and Google co-founder Larry Page. "They've kept me and the rest of the company on time and on track when it mattered most."

The OKR model has worked for Google—and hundreds of other companies.

What methodology does your company use to set and cascade goals?

SALESFORCE

Salesforce (NYSE: CRM), the pioneer of cloud computing, has 150,000 customers, including more than 400 of the Fortune 500, more than 34,000 employees, and millions of Trailblazers—the individuals and organizations who are using Salesforce to drive innovation, grow their careers and transform their businesses. Founded in 1999, they have surpassed the $10B annual run rate milestone faster than any enterprise software company in history.

Salesforce powered their amazing growth with One System.

Since their founding in 1999, this incredible company has managed the business with a system called "V2MOM" which stands for vision, values, methods, obstacles, and measures.

Even more amazing is the fact that the management system was designed by Marc Benioff, Salesforce's founder, Chairman, and Co-Chief Executive Officer. Benioff describes the system in detail in a blog post on the Salesforce website:

> "Essentially, V2MOM is an exercise in awareness in which the result is total alignment. In addition, having a clarified direction and focusing collective energy on the desired outcome eliminates the anxiety that is often present in times of change."

> "I've always thought that the biggest secret of Salesforce is how we've achieved a high level of organizational alignment and communication while growing at breakneck speeds. While a company is growing fast, there is nothing more important than constant communication and complete alignment."

> "At Salesforce, everything we do in terms of organizational management is based on our V2MOM. It is the core way we run our business; it allows us to define our goals and organize a

principled way to execute them; and it takes into consideration our constant drive to evolve. The collaborative construct works especially well for a fast-paced environment. It is challenging for every company to find a way to maintain a cohesive direction against a backdrop that is constantly changing, but V2MOM is the glue that binds us together."

High growth and complete alignment. Music to my ears!

Clearly, the system has worked. In addition to their impressive growth rate and stock performance, Salesforce has been recognized for 11 years in a row as one of Fortune's "100 Best Companies to Work For." Further, Forbes ranked Salesforce as one of the "World's Most Innovative Companies" for eight years in a row and Fortune named Salesforce one of the "Most Admired Companies" for five years in a row. They have been named a Fortune "Change the World" company for the last three years.

Standardizing on One System is a tremendous way to unleash the accelerating power of alignment. Some companies, like Salesforce, decide to build One of their own.

Does your company's planning process enable both high growth and complete alignment?

IDEXX

IDEXX Laboratories, Inc. (NASDAQ: IDXX) is a global leader in pet care innovation with over 8,000 employees serving customers in over 175 countries.

They create alignment with a comprehensive strategic planning process.

Over 68 percent of U.S. households have a pet. That translates to 80 million dogs (I have two of them), 58 million cats (sorry, but I don't like cats), and all kinds of other animals—birds, fish, snakes, and more. (I hate snakes!)

When you take your pet to the vet, there is a high probability that IDEXX's tests and equipment are used to evaluate your pet's health. They offer an extremely broad product line, organized into distinct lines of businesses, each run by a general manager.

Fast-lane companies like IDEXX use both the planning process and the codified plan to accelerate alignment.

A well-designed planning process should be the catalyst that helps your company confront the critical issues, debate potential strategies, evaluate alternatives, and allocate resources. In addition, an effective planning process "connects the dots" between the company's vision, goals, strategies, plans, and budgets.

IDEXX's Chief Financial Officer, Brian McKeon, uses an open and highly collaborative planning process to drive alignment. "We are very transparent with information," explained McKeon. "Our planning process is a byproduct of our open, cooperative culture."

The process starts each February by identifying the three or four critical strategic questions and "cross-cutting themes" that are critical to the business. Over the next few months, the executive team has multiple meetings—they call them check-ins—to discuss and unpack these questions.

"By the time we get to the multi-year plan review in May and June this up-front work and collaboration on key areas adds depth to our strategic thinking," said McKeon.

At the end of this process, they have high alignment on resource allocation priorities and key areas of execution for the annual operating plans.

IDEXX's planning process creates benefits for all stakeholders, including shareholders.

"We are proud to have built a business model with enduring and predictable growth and profit dynamics," explained Jonathan W. Ayers, IDEXX's Chairman and Chief Executive Officer. "Perhaps this is why we are part of a small minority of companies that provides earning guidance in the Q3 call for the next calendar year. Note that this has been our practice for every year for the last 15."

Clearly, McKeon's planning process has produced results. Since he joined the company in 2014, their stock has nearly quadrupled.

Who drives your company's planning process?

HAGERTY

Hagerty (www.hagerty.com) is the world's largest provider of specialty insurance to vintage vehicle enthusiasts. They employ more than 1,100 people, have offices in the United States, Canada, Germany, and the United Kingdom, and insure over 1.4 million vehicles.

They keep their car-obsessed company driving in One Direction with a One-Page Plan.

The company was started by Frank and Louise Hagerty in 1984 as an insurer of classic wooden boats. In 1991, they refocused the business on classic cars. Today, Hagerty insures everything from entry-level enthusiast vehicles to multi-million-dollar one-of-a-kind collectible cars.

McKeel Hagerty, son of Frank and Louise, took over as CEO in 1997. At the time, the company had just 50 employees. McKeel has led the company's expansion and evolution into an automotive lifestyle brand dedicated to the love and protection of driving, and the world's largest provider of specialty insurance to vintage vehicle enthusiasts.

In addition to insurance, Hagerty is now home to:

- Hagerty Drivers Club, the world's largest community for automotive enthusiasts.
- *Hagerty*, the magazine, which is among the highest circulation car magazines in the country.
- "The Barn Find Hunter," one of the most popular automobile focused shows on YouTube with nearly 700,000 subscribers.
- DriveShare, the nation's only peer-to-peer classic vehicle rental marketplace.
- MotorsportReg.com, North America's largest motorsport membership and event management system.

To keep his rapidly expanding business aligned, Hagerty implemented the "Rockefeller Habits," a management system popularized by Verne Harnish. A key component of the Rockefeller Habits system is the One-Page Strategic Plan.

Here is how Verne describes the One-Page Plan, "The bigger your company gets, and the faster it's growing, the harder it is to get everyone on the same page. The problem, of course, is that there isn't a single page around which to align."

"The Rockefeller Habits provided the framework we needed, but as we grew, we drifted away from it," explained Hagerty. "In 2017, we recommitted to the process."

Hagerty has found tremendous success with the Rockefeller Habits, but it may not be for everyone. "What you're fighting is entropy," says Hagerty. "The Rockefeller Habits, like life, require daily doses of energy to work. If a company is not prepared to 100 percent commit to executing the habits, the effectiveness can slip away."

"Our business is complex—but complexity is a choice," explained Hagerty. "The One-Page Plan allows us to create hyper-focus."

In addition, Hagerty uses software from AlignToday (www.aligntoday.com) to implement strategic alignment at scale.

While the business is intense, one of their values is "enjoy the ride." In 2018, McKeel renewed his commitment to living this and, on his days off, he can be found tooling around in one of the 25 classic cars he owns. Hagerty's first car was a red 1967 Porsche 911 S he purchased when he was 12 and restored with his dad. He still has the car. My kind of guy!

Does your plan create "hyper-focus?"

SUMMARY – ONE PLAN

Google, Salesforce, IDEXX, and Hagerty are radically different businesses. They are also wildly successful.

Planning has been a key to their success.

They implemented their plan with incredible discipline. After all, a plan without management discipline will never create alignment.

Consider the following CHECKPOINTS to evaluate your management system:

- Can you summarize your plan on One Page?

- Do you implement your plan with the required level of discipline?

- Does everyone in the company have a copy of the plan?

- How do you ensure that each person's priorities are aligned with the plan?

- Does your plan allocate resources to your highest priorities?

"It's no exaggeration to say your people managers make or break your organization's performance. They're the critical layer of connective tissue that creates alignment between the strategic priorities of your business and the employees who execute them."

Doug Dennerline
Chief Executive Officer
Betterworks

SPEED READING – EVERYONE

Every company wants everyone to be aligned.

But most are focused on engagement.

Dozens of companies have developed surveys to measure employee engagement. These are often tied to the multitude of "Best Places to Work" awards.

When you evaluate the questions in employee engagement surveys, most focus on things like company benefits, work/life balance, and the quality of the coffee.

While it is good to have employees who are engaged, it is infinitely more important that they are aligned. After all, highly engaged employees can still be driving in the wrong direction.

There are many things that you want everyone to align with. For example, you want everyone to:

- Align their behaviors with your company's code.

- Align their customer interactions with your company's brand promise.

- Align their decisions with your company's strategy.

- Align their actions with your company's way.

- Align their goals with your company's goals.

Of course, this assumes that you have clearly defined all those things.

After all, how can you hire people who are aligned with your vision if your vision is blurry? How can you train people to accomplish your mission if you don't know what it is? How can you incentivize people to deliver your brand promise if you don't have one?

That is why we have spent the last eleven chapters emphasizing the importance of clarifying those things.

In this chapter, we will explore how 23andMe, Cirque du Soleil, McKinsey, Publix, Simplexity, and the American Red Cross implemented corporate talent management disciplines to align EveryOne.

23ANDME

23andMe (www.23andme.com), based in Mountain View, California, has over 500 people and more than 5,000,000 customers. As one of the leaders in DNA testing, they have an interesting headline on their career page.

Join our gene pool.

The name 23andMe refers to the fact that human DNA is organized into 23 pairs of chromosomes. They offer a web-based service that helps people understand what their DNA says about their health, traits, and ancestry.

The process starts with a simple saliva sample. 23andMe then extracts DNA from cells in your saliva sample, processes the DNA on a genotyping chip, analyzes your genetic data, and generates a personalized report.

As you might imagine, one of their core values is "We ♡ DNA!" Here is how they explain it:

> "Deciphering the human genome is the most exciting scientific discovery of our lifetime. A secret code in each of us! There is spectacular human diversity in the world and we celebrate and embrace it. We want to empower everyone to understand the genome and what it means for each of us. We believe anyone—yes, anyone—can learn about and understand their DNA. We want to bring innovative research and products to both scientists and consumers that make them as excited about their DNA story as we are!"

Of course, they look to hire people who share their company's unique DNA:

> "It's our goal to bring innovative thinkers and top-notch talent together to make a difference in people's lives. If you're committed to our vision of

helping people access and learn from their genetic data and want to be a part of a mission-based culture, we want you to join our gene pool."

Consider this: 99.9 percent of human DNA is common to all human beings. Imagine—there are over seven billion people of all shapes, sizes, heights, weights, sexes, and colors on the planet—and our DNA is 99.9 percent alike.

Thus, only one tenth of one percent of the DNA sequence is unique to each individual.

One tenth of one percent!

We believe that each company—like each person—has a unique DNA. So, the hiring process starts with clearly identifying your company's unique DNA. While there is a standard definition for human DNA, there isn't one for corporate DNA.

In 1998, Gareth Morgan published a book called *Images of Organization*. It was the first to apply the concept of DNA to corporate culture. Since then, several other authors and consultants have also used the term with a multitude of meanings.

Whereas Blommer Chocolate's founders literally shared the same DNA, most companies must go through the process of codifying theirs. Your company's unique DNA is the thing that uniquely identifies "your kind of people."

So, to join 23andMe's "gene pool," you will have to match their unique corporate DNA.

Has your company codified your unique DNA?

CIRQUE DU SOLEIL

Cirque du Soleil (www.cirquedusoleil.com) is a global entertainment company. It has grown from an eclectic group of twenty street performers to a private-equity-owned company with over 4,000 employees, including 1,300 artists from more than 50 different countries.

Cirque du Soleil unleashed the accelerating power of alignment with One 101.

You could argue that Cirque du Soleil faces the ultimate alignment challenge:

How do you align a bunch of clowns?

Right this moment, thousands of people—none of whom are in the circus business—are thinking, "my sentiments exactly!"

Every company has a diverse workforce, but Cirque might top the list. They employ actors, singers, dancers, musicians, acrobats, gymnasts, swimmers, tumblers, jugglers, divers, mimes and, of course, clowns.

In addition, they are truly an international community, which creates unique cultural and language barriers.

All newly hired entertainers go to Cirque's International Headquarters in Montreal for preparatory training. Training can last anywhere from a few weeks to a few months.

You might think of it as Circus of the Sun 101.

Cirque's onboarding program is a full-immersion experience. Not only do the new entertainers train together, they live together in the artists' residence right across the street from headquarters.

Every company has some kind of onboarding program. For most companies, it is "hire and hope."

When you think of situations where life-or-death teamwork is required, most people think of a military environment like the Navy SEALs or the Blue Angels.

But Cirque's performances involve a high degree of risk. Therefore, their "boot camp" instills a high level of camaraderie, discipline, and trust.

Having One 101 is a key component how they align EveryOne … from Day One!

Does your company have One 101 that is mandatory for EveryOne?

P.S. I was so intrigued by this amazing company that I decided to click on the "Job Openings" link on their website. Much to my amazement, I learned that they had an opening for a "middle-aged physical actor."

So, if this alignment thing doesn't work out …

MCKINSEY AND COMPANY

McKinsey (www.mckinsey.com) is a global management consulting firm with 22 industry practices, over 12,000 consultants, 2,000 research and information professionals, and offices in 120 cities around the world.

Each year, they set aside One Day to reflect on their core values.

Here is how McKinsey describes their firm, "We are a values-driven organization. The values inform both our long-term strategy as a firm and the way we serve our clients on a daily basis."

Every company has values, but only a small subset claim that they are driven by them.

But consider McKinsey. Not only do they claim to be "values-driven," each year the entire firm takes one entire day to reflect on their values.

McKinsey makes a huge investment in Values Day. If you assume that the average billing rate for their 12,000 consultants is $500 per hour (which is probably low), the investment is in the $50M range!

How many companies do you know that believe in their values enough to invest $50M a year in them?

And if you are going to invest that kind of time and money, your values better be worth it. For your reflection, here are McKinsey's:

Adhere to the highest professional standards
- put client interests ahead of the firm's
- observe high ethical standards
- preserve client confidences
- maintain an independent perspective
- manage client and firm resources cost-effectively

Improve our clients' performance significantly
- follow the top-management approach
- use our global network to deliver the best of the firm to all clients
- bring innovations in management practice to clients
- build client capabilities to sustain improvement
- build enduring relationships based on trust

Create an unrivaled environment for exceptional people
- be nonhierarchical and inclusive
- sustain a caring meritocracy
- develop one another through apprenticeship and mentoring
- uphold the obligation to dissent
- govern ourselves as a "one firm" partnership

As you can see, their values are written according to our One Code model and contain eighteen very specific expected behaviors.

McKinsey says they are values-driven, and they put their money where their mouth is. Investing One Day per year to reflect on them is how they create strategic alignment.

Would your company take EveryOne away for an entire day just to reflect on your core values?

PUBLIX

Publix (www.publix.com) is a grocery retailer with $34 billion in sales, 1,155 stores, and 188,000 people.

They created alignment with a structure that allows EveryOne to become an owner.

Publix's late founder, George Jenkins, believed that when Publix associates were also owners, they would take care of the company and work hard to make it better.

From the start, he wanted his associates to have a stake in the company. But during the Great Depression in 1933, his associates were hardly in a position to buy stock. So, Mr. George decided to give each associate a $2-a-week raise.

That philosophy of employee ownership and profit sharing continued, and in 1951, Mr. Jenkins started the company's profit-sharing plan. In 1974, Publix created an employee stock ownership plan (ESOP).

Today, Publix is the largest employee-owned firm in America.

Any Publix associate who stays for at least a year and accrues more than 1,000 hours is granted shares of stock. Associates who remain with the company continue to receive annual grants and have the option of buying additional shares as well.

The average store manager has been with the company for over 25 years. And in May 2016, Todd Jones, a 36-year Publix veteran who started out bagging groceries, became the new CEO.

Since its inception, the company's closely held stock has risen more than 19 percent per year, twice as fast as the S&P 500 index.

In addition, Publix has racked up some impressive awards:

- Fortune's "100 Best Workplaces for Millennials"

- Fortune and the Great Place to Work Institute's "15 Best Workplaces in Retail"

- Fortune's "Most Important Private Companies"

- Fortune's "100 Best Companies to Work for in America" for 19 consecutive years

- Fortune's "Most Admired Companies" for 23 consecutive years

How much of this success is a result of being structured as an ESOP?

It is hard to attribute an exact percentage, but when every employee is an owner, the interests of the shareholders and the employees are inherently aligned.

In fact, companies with ESOPs and other broad-based employee ownership plans account for well over half of Fortune Magazine's "100 Best Companies to Work for in America" list.

There are strong business reasons to consider an ESOP as well. A study by EY found that ESOP-owned S Corporations, known as "S ESOPs" averaged 11.5 percent average annual growth compared to just 7.1 percent for the top publicly traded companies.

Publix unleashed the accelerating power of alignment with their "EveryOne is an owner" model.

Does your company share ownership with EveryOne?

SIMPLEXITY

Simplexity Product Development (www.simplexitypd.com) is a product design engineering firm with four West Coast offices.

Although they are small in size, their bonus plan creates alignment in a big—and radical—way.

It is easy to talk about aligning people with your vision, mission, and values. After all, talk is cheap.

But when it comes to using your compensation plan to create alignment, you should put your money where your mouth is.

Ever since I started working on this book (One Decade ago!), I have been looking for an exemplar company that used an innovative compensation plan to create alignment. My search ultimately led me to Simplexity. Rather than paraphrase the idea, I'd like to share excerpts of a blog written by Dorota Shortell, their Chief Executive Officer:

> "I've been thinking about whether or not to share this publicly but given the recent talk about how the working class has been largely ignored and how the rich are getting richer, I think it's my duty to speak out. I want to change the conversation and question the status quo. I've noticed that in corporate America there is often a class system. There's the executive class and then there's the working class. The executives are paid way more, get better benefits, and get big bonuses. It doesn't have to be that way.
>
> Since we are a privately held company, we get to decide how to run things. Simplexity's bonus program does not follow industry standards. Usually year-end bonuses are based on meeting certain metrics and the higher up in the organization you are, the bigger bonus you get. Or they are pro-rated

based on salary, so everyone gets, say, a 2 percent bonus. But if you make $30,000 a year, that's a $600 bonus and if you make $150,000 a year, that's a $3,000 bonus.

While there may be benefits from doing it this way, I view the annual bonus as an extra benefit for helping to contribute to the success of the team. People are already paid different salaries based on if they are an engineer or a technician, a CEO or an office assistant.

Yet every role in a company is important to meeting the goals, or it shouldn't be there in the first place. With that point-of-view, the annual bonus is a way to share the wealth.

So, here's how we set the annual bonuses at Simplexity: A certain amount of net profit (say 10 percent) is set aside in a bonus pool and then divided equally by every full-time regular employee who has worked for the company during the past year (and pro-rated for those who recently joined the company). Each person gets the same amount. That includes me as the CEO, all the executives, as well as all the technicians, and office staff. Everyone, the same dollar amount."

Yes, that's right. Every person gets exactly the same bonus. Calculate the total company bonus pool. Divide it by the number of employees you have. Write the checks. Boom!

I commend Dorota Shortell and the Simplexity team for having the courage to implement this simple—yet radical—idea. When CEOs get multi-million-dollar cash bonuses and have total compensation 1,000 times higher than the average employee, it can be hard to talk about being "One Team" with a straight face.

Does your company have a corporate bonus plan? If so, does it enhance alignment or create divisions?

AMERICAN RED CROSS

The American Red Cross (www.redcross.org) has nearly
20,000 employees and more than 370,000 volunteers.

They are thousands of people ... with One Mission.

The American Red Cross has an amazing heritage. It was
founded by Clara Barton in 1881 and has been serving
people in need ever since.

However, when Gail McGovern was appointed CEO in
2008, the organization was fragmented and in financial
distress.

Here is how McGovern described the situation, "We had
720 different chapters. Each one had a CEO. Every chapter
had their own general ledger, their own financial systems,
their own bank accounts, their own website. If you put in
'disaster relief' in Google, we wouldn't even come up
because there were 720 little websites."

In addition, they had a $209 million operating deficit and had
to borrow money just to make payroll. And to make her
challenge even greater, she was the *tenth* permanent or
interim CEO in 12 years.

McGovern developed the "One Red Cross" plan to
transform the organization. The plan included six strategic
initiatives: achieving financial stability, increasing donations,
improving blood services quality, revitalizing the Red Cross
brand, modernizing IT systems, and promoting teamwork.

Creating a "One Company" culture is always challenging,
but it is probably ten times harder in volunteer-powered
organizations.

Prior to joining the Red Cross, McGovern was a professor at
the Harvard Business School. Before joining HBS, she held
senior executive positions at AT&T and Fidelity
Investments. While she was clearly a highly regarded and

accomplished executive, leading volunteers required her to develop new leadership skills.

"In the corporate world, people jump when the CEO says so. At Red Cross, I would say jump … and the volunteers asked why?" she explained. "So, I had to create alignment through the power of my ideas, not the power of my office."

The transformation of the Red Cross required massive changes. Like any change initiative, there was some resistance. Overcoming this resistance required persistence, fortitude, constant communication, and an outstanding team.

McGovern shared a key insight about her experience: "People don't hate change … they hate uncertainty." But ultimately, she found that "Red Crossers were willing to make whatever changes were necessary to save the Red Cross and its life-saving mission."

Since implementing the One Red Cross plan, the organization has become financially stable, more efficient, more agile, and more aligned.

The first exemplar we studied was Alan Mulally's remarkable transformation of Ford. I think it is fitting that our last exemplar is Gail McGovern's similarly remarkable transformation of the American Red Cross.

Both leaders were outsiders brought in to turn around proud, century-old institutions. Both leaders inherited highly fragmented organizations that were in deep financial trouble. Both used the accelerating power of alignment to get their organizations driving in One Direction.

Does your company operate as One Company?

SUMMARY – EVERYONE

Accelerator Number One focused on aligning the executive team.

This One focused on aligning EveryOne!

Perhaps more than any other business function, corporate talent management has the power to improve alignment. In this chapter, we explored how exemplar companies did it.

23andMe is looking for people who share their DNA to join their "gene pool." Cirque du Soleil uses their One 101 to align a bunch of clowns. McKinsey invests One Day to reflect on their values. Publix creates alignment with the ESOP that allows EveryOne to become an owner. Simplexity's "radical" bonus system pays EveryOne the same amount. The American Red Cross had the unique challenge of aligning both employees and volunteers.

How about your company? Consider the following CHECKPOINTS to evaluate your company's talent management:

- Are you focused on employee engagement or employee alignment?

- How do you ensure that you only hire the "right" people?

- Does your onboarding process create alignment from Day One?

- Would your company take EveryOne away for an entire day just to reflect on your values?

- What other talent management disciplines do you leverage to create alignment?

SUMMARY
PART TWO

THE
ACCELERATORS

SUMMARY – THE ACCELERATORS

In **Part Two – *The Twelve Accelerators***, we introduced the twelve components of the ***Drive One Direction*®** methodology and explored how fifty exemplar companies applied them.

Which of the exemplar cases was your favorite?

We started with One Team—because a misaligned executive team will never create an aligned company.

Then, we looked at ten other components. One Thing. One Vision. One Mission. One Code. One Brand. One Strategy. One Portfolio. One Way. One Wow! One Plan.

Finally, we explored how companies applied the discipline of talent management to align EveryOne—because while alignment starts with One Team, you can't win unless you align EveryOne.

These are twelve components of your corporate core. The stronger your core, the more successful you will be. A strong corporate core is like a stabilizing centripetal force that keeps everyone—and everything—aligned.

You don't develop six-pack abs because you did some sit-ups three years ago. Likewise, you don't create a strong corporate core because you printed some core values posters three years ago.

Developing a strong corporate core is essential. The stronger your corporate core, the faster your company can grow.

While we believe that each Accelerator is important, they may not be equally important. Improving some of them might be urgent, while others can wait.

To develop your roadmap, use the following 3x3 matrix:

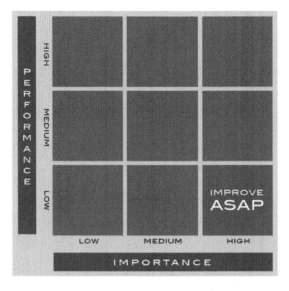

On the vertical axis, categorize each Accelerator based on your current performance: High, Medium, and Low. On the horizontal axis, categorize them in terms of their strategic importance: High, Medium, and Low.

Plotting each of the Accelerators on this 3x3 matrix will enable you to visualize your current situation and prioritize your alignment roadmap.

If you have items in the lower right quadrant, these must be addressed first. These are both highly important and underperforming.

Finally, while we covered twelve of the most important Accelerators, your company might have additional One(s). For example, if board alignment is an issue, you should strive to create One Board. If channel alignment is important, create One Channel.

Once you have evaluated each One, consolidate your alignment initiatives into One Roadmap.

SELECT ONE BIG ONE

Another insight from the exemplar companies is that they put most of their "alignment energy" into One Big One.

We strongly recommend that you follow their example.

So, while we recommend that you implement all the Accelerators in the **Drive One Direction®** methodology, your company should consider an intense focus on One Big One.

As a reminder, here are some of the One Big Ones that the exemplars use:

- For McKinsey and Company, it is their values.

- For BTI360, it is their One Thing.

- For Bognet Construction, it is The BOGNET Way.

- For Amazon, it is their Day One Obsession.

- For Virgin, it is their One Brand.

- For TOMS, it is their One for One business model.

- For Dollar Tree, it is their One Price Point pricing strategy.

- For USAA, it is their unmatched focus on One Market.

These exemplars elevated One to be The Big One.

But for it to be "The One," it must pass five simple tests:

First, it must be clear.

Second, it must be compelling.

Third, it must be inspiring.

Fourth, since you must align everyone—and everything—with it, your One Big One must be unifying.

Finally, your One Big One should also differentiate your company from all your competitors.

Clear. Compelling. Inspiring. Unifying. Differentiating.

This is how your One Big One can become your competitive differentiation. It both unifies your company *and* differentiates you from everyone else.

For example, hundreds of companies do construction, but only One builds The Bognet Way.

Hundreds of companies sell insurance, but only USAA is focused exclusively on the military.

Hundreds of companies sell shoes. But only TOMS sells them the One for One Way.

If you can develop One Big One, you will be on the way to greatness.

PART THREE

DRIVE

ONE

DIRECTION

1	ONE TEAM
2	ONE THING
3	ONE VISION
4	ONE MISSION
5	ONE CODE
6	ONE BRAND
7	ONE STRATEGY
8	ONE PORTFOLIO
9	ONE WAY
10	ONE WOW!
11	ONE PLAN
12	EVERYONE

DRIVE

ONE

DIRECTION

ALIGNMENT IS THE ULTIMATE COMPETITIVE ADVANTAGE

SPEED READING – DRIVE ONE DIRECTION

Hopefully, you have developed your One Roadmap and selected your One Big One.

Now it is time to use those to transform and align your company.

In **Part Three – *Drive One Direction***, we will explore The Twelve Disciplines. These are twelve best practices that exemplar companies have used to unleash the accelerating power of alignment.

Much has been written about the process of leading change and the high percentage of corporate change initiatives that fail.

We believe that alignment is a special type of change. Therefore, creating alignment needs a special type of change management process.

These are The Twelve Disciplines:

1. Make Alignment Job One.

2. Run a One-Company Campaign.

3. Build a One-Company Culture.

4. Develop One System.

5. Leverage One Model: Debate, Decide, and Align.

6. Deliver One Message.

7. Apply One Process.

8. Work as One.

9. Utilize One Style.

10. Meet One-on-One.

11. Plan on One Decade.

12. Start with One Person.

If I had to summarize the process of creating alignment with just one symbol, it would be the curly bracket. That is why we use it as shorthand for the **Drive One Direction**® methodology.

The Twelve Disciplines will provide the } you need to transform and align your company.

MAKE ALIGNMENT JOB ONE

As you surely know by now, we believe that alignment is the ultimate competitive advantage. If you share that conviction, then creating alignment is not a tangential, tertiary, nice-to-have issue for your company. It is mission-critical.

Otherwise known as Job One.

The exemplar companies completely embraced this idea.

Of course, this starts with the CEO.

During my interview with Alan Mulally, he actually used our tagline, "Alignment is the ultimate competitive advantage."

Randy Papadellis, operated as Ocean Spray's "Chief Alignment Officer."

The founders of The Carlyle Group were so convinced of the importance of alignment that they codified the "One Carlyle" message from Day One.

Gail McGovern's unwavering commitment to being "One Red Cross" was the key to their amazing turnaround.

Linda Chadwick, the Chief Executive Officer of Rita's Water Ice, explained this emphatically, "Getting everyone going in the same direction is my Number One Priority."

The executive team must embrace this idea as well. They must truly believe that alignment is mission critical.

Too often, we see passive "lip service" commitments to alignment initiatives. People *say* that alignment is Job One, but their actions deliver a different message.

We recommend that companies use assessment tools like the SHIFTPOINTS Corporate Alignment Percentage or the Acceleration Index to quantify the their current level of alignment.

We also suggest that companies use those metrics to calculate the true cost of misalignment. For most, this will be a startlingly high number.

Once you have quantified the cost of misalignment, improving it will surely be One of your priorites ... but will it be Number One?

It seems redundant to say, "One Number One Priority," but some companies have so many priorities that everything is a priority. Too often, companies even have competing, contradictory priorities.

Bill Pollard, the retired chairman of ServiceMaster, was talking with Peter Drucker about priorities. Peter said, "Bill, it wasn't until the 20th century that we pluralized the word priority. For most of its history, the word has been singular."

So, if you can only have One Number One Priority, what should it be? We obviously think that Alignment must be Job One.

To turn alignment into a competitive advantage, it must be Job One.

RUN A ONE-COMPANY CAMPAIGN

If your company is massively misaligned, you may need a One-Company Campaign.

Before you decide, remember that many people are jaded, cynical, skeptical, and distrustful of these kinds of initiatives.

And that is on a good day.

Nonetheless, should you decide to implement a One-Company campaign, your company should employ several best practices, including:

- **Inspire results with relentless, unwavering leadership.** Alignment does not just happen. It takes lots of hard work and an intentional focus on the issue.

- **Manage alignment with a high-powered A-Team.** The Alignment Team will manage the alignment process. (Some companies call this a program management office, or PMO.) They must have the organizational credibility and political capital to build coalitions and break down barriers.

- **Create excitement with a high-energy launch.** One way to accelerate results is to launch the change with town hall meetings, e-mail blasts, videos, web content, posters, banners, and the obligatory T-shirts. While these elements can be fun, their impact is short-term. So, launch with fanfare, but sustain the effort. And remember, many people are cynical about these kinds of things. Don't be lame.

- **Accelerate alignment by leveraging key influencers.** It is essential to have key influencers, both internal and external, on board with the program. Find and empower your early adopters.

These people "get it" right away, and incorporating their suggestions is critical to accelerating success.

- **Visualize progress with a war room that dramatizes the change.** This is a fantastic tool for highlighting misalignment. This can be especially helpful when your company has lots of "old versions" of things. Use a progress wall so everyone can see the before and after.

- **Build endurance with a steady stream of wins and validations.** Delivering early wins is a must. Celebrating them publicly will generate momentum, but avoid declaring victory too early. Many programs start out well but hit the wall. Easy issues are resolved first; difficult ones are procrastinated. Success requires endurance.

- **Drive progress with a clear project timeline, roadmap, and deadlines.** Often, this means going faster than most think is possible or prudent. Some may worry about the timeline being too aggressive, but our experience is that organizations can change a lot faster than they think they can.

- **Run the transformation in 90-Day SPRINTS.** SHIFTPOINTS has had tremendous success with the 90-day SPRINT model. Start by breaking the transformation into specific initiatives that can be accomplished within 90 days. Meet at the start of every quarter to review progress. Color-code each initiative with red, yellow, or green to indicate whether it has been accomplished.

These best practices will improve the probability of success.

BUILD A ONE-COMPANY CULTURE

Every company has a culture.

But most have a dysfunctional one.

The Three Musketeers is a novel by Alexandre Dumas set in seventeenth-century Paris. It tells the story of a young man named d'Artagnan who wants to join the Musketeers of the Guard.

The Three Musketeers made the phrase "all for one and one for all" famous ("tous pour un, et un pour tous").

All for One and One for All.

This sounds a lot easier than it is. Unfortunately, the cultural dynamic we often see is "All for me and none for you!"

Companies actually have dozens of cultures.

The accounting team has a culture. The European sales team has one. The manufacturing plant has a different one.

The key is to build a One-Company culture that unifies and aligns everyone.

Unfortunately, Bain & Company research found that only 10 percent of companies have a high-performance culture.

While there are many reasons for this, one of the most dysfunctional is infighting.

Sometimes, this behavior is demonstrated in the budgeting process, which is often managed as a zero-sum game. Sometimes, it manifests itself in unhealthy internal competition and power struggles.

Peter Drucker famously said that "culture eats strategy for breakfast." That sounds good, but I am not sure it is true.

What is true is that companies with One-Company cultures can leverage the full breadth and depth of the firm to win and serve customers. These highly aligned companies eat their fragmented and dysfunctional competitors for breakfast … lunch … and dinner!

Ideally, your company has built the One-Company mindset into your culture from Day One.

If, however, you have allowed your culture to disintegrate into warring tribes and dysfunctional fiefdoms, you have a lot of work to do.

Does your company have a One-Company culture?

DEVELOP ONE SYSTEM

Every company has a system for managing the business.

But most are not particularly systematized.

When your company is small, managing it is relatively easy.

As you grow, complexity increases exponentially. To effectively manage the business, companies must create a management system.

In the classic *Harvard Business Review* article, "Mastering the Management System," professors Robert S. Kaplan and David P. Norton describe the need for a management system:

> "In our experience, however, breakdowns in a company's management system, not managers' lack of ability or effort, are what cause a company's underperformance. By management system, we're referring to the integrated set of processes and tools that a company uses to develop its strategy, translate it into operational actions, and monitor and improve the effectiveness of both."

There are dozens of different management systems. Some of the most popular ones include:

- The balanced scorecard, developed by Harvard Business School professors Robert S. Kaplan and David P. Norton

- Objectives and key results (OKRs), developed by Andy Grove at Intel

- "The Rockefeller Habits," developed by Verne Harnish

- "The Entrepreneurial Operating System," developed by Geno Wickman and Don Tinney

- "Holocracy," developed by Holocracy One

- "The Top Gear System," developed by SHIFTPOINTS

- And many others

Each of these systems can be effective, but we advise clients to pick One of them. When a company adopts One System as your Alignment Management System, it provides a common language, which speeds communication and reduces friction.

Does your company have One Alignment Management System?

LEVERAGE ONE MODEL

To improve alignment, your executive team will likely have to deal with tough, deep-seated issues.

We strongly recommend that you use the "debate, decide, and align" model.

One of the most dysfunctional and destructive organizational pathologies is "undermining."

Unfortunately, we see this all the time.

Issues are discussed at the executive meeting. Alternatives are debated. And eventually, a decision about the best course of action is made.

Far too often, what happens next is that executives who did not get their way undermine the decision. Sometimes, their undermining is overt, blatant, and public, such as when executives tell their direct reports, "*They* made a dumb decision."

Most of the time, however, the undermining is much more covert. Whispering at the watercooler. Backstabbing in the bathroom. Sniping at Starbucks.

This kind of behavior, especially at executive levels, must never be tolerated.

High-performance executive teams use the "debate, decide, and align" model. Once a decision is made, everyone aligns behind it, even it if wasn't their preferred course of action.

I recognize that this is difficult. Most people can't simply turn a switch and become passionate champions for an idea they vehemently disagreed with.

We once worked with a company that was grinding through the process of selecting their One Number.

First, there was a debate about whether using One Number to improve alignment was a good idea or not. Frankly, some executives thought it was unnecessary. Eventually, the CEO decided that it would indeed help the company improve alignment.

Once the CEO decided to do it, there was another debate about which number to choose. Then, there was another debate about the formula they would use to calculate their One Number. Then, there was yet another debate about what the target should be.

That is why creating alignment can be exhausting.

Ultimately, we came to a decision. We would use One Number. We agreed on One Formula and One Target. We launched the idea in a company-wide campaign.

Unfortunately, one executive (who was part of the entire process) refused to comply. Every time he showed his metric in company meetings, he used his own (non-compliant) formula. This was blatant, intentional undermining.

I would have fired him, but the CEO was reluctant to do so because his division was the most profitable one.

Alignment is a choice. And so is undermining.

In some cases, the undermining is intentional and volitional. In other cases, it is passive-aggressive.

Sometimes, the underminer is a single individual, acting alone. In other cases, it is led by a group or coalition. (We once facilitated an executive team offsite where a group of executives came into the meeting with the expressed purpose of leading a mutiny against the CEO.)

You should use the "debate, decide, and align" model to address critical alignment issues.

DELIVER ONE MESSAGE

In addition to optimizing each One, you must take the additional step of looking at them holistically.

They must deliver One Message.

This extra step ensures that each of your One(s) is aligned with each other—and this step is critical.

Every research study confirms that most employees are disengaged. One root cause for disengaged employees is something we call "corporate hypocrisy." This takes place when the company's words, actions, policies, decisions, and behaviors don't match.

In our experience, mixed messages kill alignment.

Awhile back, I worked with a sales executive who had cut his teeth in a hard-core door-to-door sales organization.

The company sold coupons for automotive repair services. Each representative would knock on hundreds of doors every day, facing mindboggling levels of rejection.

Although I have had hundreds of hours of sales training, he taught me something I had never heard before: *"The confused mind always says no."*

The corollary for leaders is, "The confused employee always shifts into neutral."

To prevent your employees from shifting into neutral, you must deliver One Message.

First, your words must be aligned. Your vision must align with your brand promise. Your mission must align with your values. Your executives must speak with One Voice.

Second, your actions must be aligned with your words.

You can't proclaim that you value diversity and have twelve white men on the board. You can't talk about being One Team and tolerate undermining. You can't promise One Wow! and not deliver it.

The **Drive One Direction®** methodology is an integrated system. Ensuring that everything is aligned to deliver One Message is a critical step in the process.

You can't win the race if confused employees shift into neutral.

APPLY ONE PROCESS

A few years ago, I took a trip to Napa Valley, California, and learned an important lesson about alignment.

The best wine comes from the vines that have been aggressively pruned.

In order to unleash the accelerating power of alignment, your company must also apply the discipline of pruning. For example, you must:

- Prune initiatives that are out of alignment with your mission.

- Prune executives who are out of alignment with your values.

- Prune products that are out of alignment with your strategy.

- Prune messages that are out of alignment with your campaign.

The discipline of pruning allows you to shed the things—and people—that hinder your progress.

Harvard Business School professor Michael Watkins has a great way of explaining this idea, "If 'the essence of strategy is choosing what not to do,' as Michael Porter famously said in a seminal HBR article, then the essence of execution is truly not doing it. That sounds simple, but it's surprisingly hard for organizations to kill existing initiatives, even when they don't align with new strategies."

Is your company struggling with the strategy of "more"? Do you suffer from "initiative creep"?

We once worked with a large nonprofit organization. They had just launched a major transformational initiative but were struggling to get everyone—and everything—aligned with it.

I asked the CEO, "Since launching the campaign, what have you *stopped* doing?"

His answer was, "Ummmm … nothing."

One of the reasons we use the word "One" all the time is that it forces companies to ruthlessly prioritize.

Every goal is important … which is the most important One?

In addition, when you evaluate everything from the perspective of total alignment, you identify the cost of even small levels of misalignment.

When a division is 80 percent aligned with your strategy, it is still 20 percent misaligned. When a team is 90 percent bought-in to your vision, they are still 10 percent opted-out. If your delivery is just 5 percent misaligned with your brand promise, you will have a lot of unhappy customers.

My hunch is that you have people—and things—in your company that are far more misaligned than that.

You must have the courage—and the discipline—to confront and prune them if necessary.

Just like wine, the best results come from the companies that are aggressively pruned.

WORK AS ONE

Box (NYSE: BOX) is an enterprise content management platform that securely connects people, information, and applications. More than 41 million users—including SHIFTPOINTS—trust Box to manage content in the cloud.

Their new advertising campaign is entitled, "Work as One."

Obviously, that caught my attention.

This chapter is not about Box per se, but about the incredible power of technology to improve alignment. An entire book could be written about this, but I will cover some of the highlights in One Chapter.

As part of the research for this book, I interviewed many software company executives, who provided insights that were extremely helpful. These companies literally go from A to Z, so I would like to thank them in alphabetical order:

- AchieveIt

- AlignToday

- Atiim

- Box.com

- Betterworks

- Lattice

- Slack

- The Predictive Index

- Workboard

- Zoom

These companies are leveraging their technology expertise to solve the alignment problem. (I love how Zoom describes their value proposition, "More Teams. Less Work.")

As we explained in the One Generation chapter, technology has changed the world. In addition, cloud-based tools have enabled cloud-based companies to change the rules of business. For example, Automattic and Zapier are 100 percent virtual. (Another A to Z!). These companies invest in cloud-based technologies in lieu of office space to create alignment.

Most companies, however, have a hybrid model. Some of their employees are in physical company offices, others are full-time teleworkers, and others are road warriors whose office is often a Starbucks or an airport lounge.

Whether your company has One Person or One Million, aligning everyone—and everything—is mission-critical. These new cloud-based tools provide a great new way to do it.

I strongly recommend that you contact these companies to learn how technology can help your team "Work as One."

UTILIZE ONE STYLE

Microsoft (NASDAQ: MSFT) is an impressive company with a proud history. Although their headquarters is at One Microsoft Way, the company was notorious for its silos.

The Microsoft case is a great lesson on importance of leadership style.

In July 2013, Microsoft CEO Steve Ballmer announced a company-wide reorganization called "One Microsoft." The plan was developed during a meeting at a Starbucks with Alan Mulally, who was still the CEO of Ford at that time.

Here is how Ballmer tried to sell the idea, "All of this means that we need to move forward as one Microsoft with one strategy and one set of goals. We'll have one approach to the marketplace, whether it's business partners, innovation partners, developers, IT people, or consumers. We'll have one technology base to enable us in core areas as opposed to two or more. We're one Microsoft."

Clearly, Ballmer was highly influenced by the success of Mulally's ONE FORD plan. But it was too little, too late. Six weeks later, Ballmer announced his resignation.

Satya Nadella became the CEO of Microsoft in February 2014. He decided to give the One Microsoft idea another try.

Here is how he sold the vision. "We are one company, one Microsoft—not a confederation of fiefdoms. Innovation and competition don't respect our silos, so we have to learn to transcend those barriers. It's our ability to work together that makes our dreams believable and, ultimately, achievable."

By all accounts, Nadella is succeeding where Ballmer failed. The stock has more than tripled during his tenure so far.

Why?

When it comes to creating alignment, leadership style really matters. Nadella's collaborative style, his inspiring personal story, and his deep credibility within Microsoft were keys to his success.

There are hundreds of books on leading change—but alignment is a special type of change and therefore requires a special style of leadership.

You lead change, but you inspire alignment.

Many of the exemplar companies we studied are also Best Places to Work winners. These companies are led by servant leaders. These servant leaders create environments where people align because they want to, not because they were forced to.

When I went to work at IBM in 1979, wearing a white shirt to work was essentially mandatory. Even though it was not a formal written policy, it was a key component of their culture and brand identity.

I loved IBM. I loved what it stood for. I was proud to work there. My parents were proud that I worked there.

I wore blue suits, white shirts, and "Captain America" ties to work every day because I wanted to, not because I had to.

In our exemplar companies, people enthusiastically and willingly align. They recognize that the standards are set to help them reach a higher ground, not just to force conformity to some ill-conceived program from corporate.

Ultimately, people align because they are inspired, not because it is required.

MEET ONE-ON-ONE

Alignment is a contact sport.

Every manager has a role to play.

Many exemplar companies have institutionalized One-on-One meetings. They are an exceptional way to optimize alignment.

This short meeting, held once per week, can "connect the dots" between your corporate strategy, goals, plans, and initiatives and every employee's individual activities.

Ideally, this starts at the top. The CEO should have One-on-Ones with their direct reports to model the behavior. The executive team should do the same.

Here are some questions that managers can use to turn One-on-One meetings into alignment meetings:

- Do you think our vision is inspiring?

- What do our core values mean to you?

- Do you understand our corporate strategy?

- How do your goals align with our corporate goals?

- What can we do to improve teamwork and collaboration?

- Do you see any areas of misalignment that should be addressed?

Obviously, there are hundreds of other questions.

One-on-One meetings are just one component of the process known as Continuous Performance Management® (CPM).

One of the benefits of Continuous Performance Management is that it allows companies to increase strategic agility. Fast-lane companies are revising their strategy and goals quarterly. When you develop strategy four times faster, you can respond four times faster … assuming that your company can dynamically realign everyone—and everything—to capitalize.

The second benefit of CPM is that individual performance improves. The discipline of regular One-on-One meetings, structured conversations, and improved coaching produces dramatic results. According to McKinsey, 68 percent of respondents agree that ongoing coaching and feedback conversations have a positive impact on individual performance.

Imagine a company where 100 percent of the people invest 100 percent of their energy in activities that are 100 percent aligned with the strategic plan. Imagine being able to quickly realign the entire company to capitalize on new opportunities or respond to competitive threats. Then, imagine having real-time analytics to measure and optimize goal alignment.

Fast-lane companies are leveraging the power of One-on-One meetings to accelerate alignment. In addition, new technology from companies mentioned in the Work as One chapter can help automate the process and give HR professionals a way to hold managers accountable for having them.

One-on-One meetings are an important component of driving your company in One Direction.

NOTE: Continuous Performance Management® is a registered trademark of Betterworks.

PLAN ON ONE DECADE

In *Part One – Alignment 101*, we explored the radical changes that have happened in the workforce in just One Generation.

Alignment is radically harder than it was One Generation ago.

Therefore, companies must be much more sophisticated and intentional about creating alignment. That is why we developed the *Drive One Direction*® methodology.

The process starts with One Team.

But it never ends. Alignment is not a One-and-Done process.

One of the key insights from the exemplars was how consistent they were.

Johnson & Johnson has lived by their One Credo for over seventy years. GEICO has been using One Tagline for over fifteen years. Bognet Construction has been building The BOGNET Way for over ten years.

Amazon has been guided by their One Obsession since Day One.

Unfortunately, most companies do not have the discipline to stay with their One-Company Campaign long enough for it to actually create alignment.

Too often, what we see is more akin to the "Idea of the Month Club."

Often, this comes from the top. Every time the CEO reads a new book or attends a new seminar, there is a new initiative. Rather than making a long-term commitment to One Idea, they have "One-Night Stands" with all of them.

We once worked with a company that wanted to Evolve! their company. It was supposed to be a long-term alignment campaign. They gave up after six months.

This kind of herky-jerky leadership makes employees reach for the barf bags!

In contrast, fast-lane companies understand the importance of consistency. It takes unwavering leadership and irrational perseverance to create strategic alignment.

Most companies want a quick fix. Unfortunately, it just doesn't work that way.

START WITH ONE PERSON

Most of this book has been about corporate alignment. All that corporate stuff is fine, but alignment ultimately starts with One Person.

You.

Perhaps you are the CEO of your company. Then, *please* be the Chief Alignment Officer.

If you are a member of the corporate executive team, *please* work as One Team and make alignment Job One.

But regardless of your position, you must make a decision.

You can either be a force for unity, or you can be a force for division.

That is because alignment is a decision.

You can decide to undermine, or you can decide to align.

You can opt-out, or you can buy-in.

You can be "me me me," or you can put "we before me."

You can drive the decelerating power of division, or you can unleash the accelerating power of alignment.

Which will you choose?

Imagine a company where everyone is aligned.

How amazing would it be to come to work every day and know that your team is 100 percent aligned with you—and that you are 100 percent aligned with them?

Live the core values. Implement the strategy. Deliver the brand promise.

If your team is aligned, you can overcome any obstacle. If EveryOne is aligned, your company can accomplish anything.

Hold yourself accountable. Hold other people accountable.

Look for things that are out of alignment and fix them. If you see a document with the old vision statement, fix it.

Yes, there are challenges. Yes, there are obstacles to overcome. Yes, there are processes to be optimized. There are customer complaints to satisfy.

What I am saying is that the best way to overcome obstacles, optimize processes, and satisfy customers is to work as One Team. To rally around One Vision.

To be One Company … driving in One Direction.

SUMMARY – DRIVE ONE DIRECTION

Alignment is just One Word.

But describing the process for turning it into a competitive advantage took over 40,000 of them!

In **Part One – *Alignment 101***, we covered The Twelve Foundational Principles of alignment.

In **Part Two – *The Twelve Accelerators***, we introduced the twelve components of the ***Drive One Direction*®** methodology. We also explored how fifty exemplar companies used those components.

In **Part Three – *Drive One Direction***, we covered The Twelve Disciplines … these are best practices that your company should use to transform and align your organization.

I hope we have convinced you that alignment is the ultimate competitive advantage. I hope you were inspired by the exemplar companies we studied. I hope you are now committed to being an alignment champion for your company.

While alignment is incredibly powerful, it can be difficult to attain.

Unfortunately, the issues associated with creating alignment often fall in the "important, but not urgent" category.

In addition, they often require difficult conversations that many executive teams would rather sweep under the rug.

Therefore, they are *exactly* the kinds of issues that are well suited for an independent and objective outsider who has no stake in the outcome. Someone who can challenge assumptions and ask the "elephant in the room" questions.

SHIFTPOINTS plays that role for our clients. We have several offerings that can accelerate the alignment process:

- **The Acceleration Index**™. An assessment of your company's alignment based on the *Drive One Direction*® methodology.

- **The Navigation Index**™. An assessment of your executive team based on the *Develop One Team* methodology.

- **The Jump Start Program**™. A keynote speech, delivered by yours truly, that will inspire your team to align.

- **The Pit Stop Program**®. A 90-day engagement that culminates in an executive offsite meeting. The sole purpose of the Pit Stop Program is to help companies develop a roadmap to unleash the accelerating power of alignment.

- **The Top Gear Program**™. A long-term coaching program designed specifically for Chief Alignment Officers and executive teams.

- **The SHIFTPOINTS Blog.** The blog is written in the same punchy style as the book. Postings are designed to be read in 60 seconds. Otherwise known as One Minute! Fast. Informative. Provocative. And hopefully entertaining.

Leading transformational alignment initiatives is not for the faint of heart, but as Home Depot used to say:

You can do it. We can help.

To learn more, contact us at start@SHIFTPOINTS.com.

"The road to real alignment is often paved with conflict. Feigning consensus is never the solution—rather, it's accepting and addressing conflict in a strategic way."

David Novak
Former Chairman and CEO
Yum! Brands

ONE FORD – THE EXPECTED BEHAVIORS

Alan Mulally suggested that I include Ford's Sixteen Expected Behaviors in the book.

When Alan suggests something, I do it!

These behaviors are organized into four sections, which are then summarized with the acrostic FORD.

Foster Functional and Technical Excellence:

- Know and have a passion for our business and our customers

- Demonstrate and build functional and technical excellence

- Ensure process discipline

- Have a continuous improvement philosophy and practice

Own Working Together:

- Believe in skilled and motivated people working together

- Include everyone; respect, listen to, help and appreciate others

- Build strong relationships; be a team player; develop ourselves and others

- Communicate clearly, concisely and candidly

Role Model Ford Values:

- Show initiative, courage, integrity and good corporate citizenship

- Improve quality, safety and sustainability

- Have a can do, find a way attitude and emotional resilience

- Enjoy the journey and each other; have fun—never at others' expense

Deliver Results:

- Deal positively with our business realities; develop compelling and comprehensive plans, while keeping an enterprise view

- Set high expectations and inspire others

- Make sound decisions using facts and data

- Hold ourselves and others responsible and accountable for delivering results and satisfying our customers

These behaviors were an important part of creating a One Ford culture.

ONE LIFE STAGE

Alignment is mission-critical.

However, how you create it and how much you need is a function of what stage your company is in.

Below is a list of ten common company stages. Which One are you in?

Startup
Some startups develop a strong sense of alignment from Day One. Most, however, are so focused on survival that wordsmithing a mission statement seems like a big waste of time. Regardless, the primary alignment issue for companies in the Startup stage is product/market fit.

Scale-up
Scale-ups have built a viable enterprise but are still primarily focused on One Core Product and One Core Market. The primary alignment issue for Scale-Ups is focus. They must fight the temptation to diversify too much and too soon.

Expansion
Expansion-stage companies are expanding beyond One Core Product and One Core Market. Companies in this stage are starting to add divisions. They might also be adding additional geographic offices. The primary alignment issue for companies in the Expansion stage is building a One-Company mindset before the divisions create division.

Reenergize
Companies in the Reenergize stage have plateaued and need to get the company growing again. The primary alignment issue for companies in the Reenergize stage is getting back to their core—they must prune the distractions.

Realign
Companies in the Realign stage are fragmented and dysfunctional. They have silos and warring tribes. They

must confront tough issues and deeply ingrained dysfunctional behaviors—often within the executive team.

Spin Out
Companies in the Spin Out stage are being spun out from a corporate parent. They will have a new company name and a new brand. Their primary alignment challenge is to keep the best from their corporate parent and, at the same time, develop their own unique way of creating alignment.

Consolidation
Companies in the Consolidation stage are shedding non-core assets so they can refocus on their core business. As divisions are sold, it is hard to maintain employee goodwill. Once the consolidation is completed, companies must align the remaining employees with the new vision and strategy.

Transformation
Companies in the Transformation stage have old core businesses that have stagnated. They are focused on creating new ones. For many companies, this is seen as a "digital" transformation, but transformations can come in many forms. The primary alignment issue is maintaining the existing core business while liberating the new one.

Makeover
Makeover companies are solid, but tired. The primary alignment issue for companies in the Makeover stage is establishing a new brand identity. It can be very difficult to change—aka realign—what customers think of you.

Integration
After a merger, the challenge is to make One Company out of two. Integration-stage companies literally have two of everything—two mission statements, two lists of core values, two accounting systems, etc.—and they must consolidate down to One. Companies in this stage have thousands of alignment issues.

Which life stage is your company in? How does that impact how you create alignment?

ONE OPERATING MODEL

Companies operate in many ways. Some are highly centralized, others are highly decentralized.

Your corporate operating model is a key factor in deciding how to create alignment.

The following list is not meant to be exhaustive but can help you articulate your operating model.

The "One Business" Company
- Company competes primarily in One Market
- Most likely, the company is organized functionally (sales, marketing, manufacturing, etc.)
- Most likely, there is One P&L

The Highly Centralized Corporation
- Big, strong corporate headquarters
- Most of the big decisions are made at corporate
- Divisions are partially autonomous
- Alignment is primarily created "top-down" by corporate

The Multidivisional Corporation
- Strong corporate headquarters and strong divisions
- Division leaders are General Managers
- An even balance of power between corporate and divisions
- Cross-divisional alignment is created by corporate

The Federation
- Moderately strong corporate headquarters
- Autonomous divisions, often led by Presidents
- Only a small amount of "top-down" corporate-level alignment
- Alignment is primarily created at the divisional level
- Small focus on cross-divisional alignment

The Conglomeration—A Company of Companies

- Small corporate headquarters
- Company Presidents are highly autonomous
- Alignment is primarily created at the operating company level
- Little or no focus on cross-company alignment

The Association
- Corporate has very little power
- Members choose to affiliate—or not
- Members pay to be a part of the association
- Corporate has limited decision authority, and primarily exists to serve the members
- Alignment is often around a common agenda

The Denomination
- Many different operating models
- Some have very strong corporate-driven alignment … others have very little
- Always bound together by One Doctrine and/or One Tradition

The Abomination
- If your company is in this category, you definitely need this book!

What is your company's operating model?

ONE BOOK

I've written four books and have read hundreds of them.

But Only One Book changed my life.

I did not grow up going to church. In the sixth grade, I had a bad experience with the Catholic Church and swore off religion.

In high school, I read Mark Twain's *Letters from Earth* and decided that I was an atheist.

After college, I started dating a beautiful Vietnamese girl named Twee, only to learn that she was a pastor's daughter. (We've been married since 1985.)

She challenged me to read the Bible for myself. Of course, I did not own a copy, so she bought me my First One.

I started reading it but got bogged down in Leviticus. I explained this to Twee. Her response? "You should read the New Testament."

To which I replied, "Then why did you buy me the old one?"

Such was my level of biblical illiteracy.

Besides, what kind of book starts over three-quarters of the way through?

The Bible is the best-selling book in history, with total sales exceeding five billion copies.

Interestingly, it is also the most shoplifted book as well.

The Bible is One Book, but it contains sixty-six books. They were written on three continents by forty different people over a period of 1,500 years.

The Bible was originally written in three languages (Hebrew, Aramaic, and Greek). It has now been translated into almost three thousand other languages.

The shortest chapter in the Bible is Psalm 117. The longest chapter is Psalm 119. And Psalm 118 is the middle chapter of the entire Bible.

How's that for intelligent design?

Psalm 118 verse 8 is the middle verse of the entire Bible.

"It is better to take refuge in the Lord than to trust man."

That is a nice One Sentence Summary of the entire book.

I hope you liked my book. I hope it helps your company be more aligned.

But my One Wish is for you to read the Bible for yourself.

Maybe it will change your life, too.

I have just One Suggestion: start with the New Testament.

ONE PLATFORM

Our last chapter touched the touchy subject of religion.

So, to heck with it … I might as well write about politics as well.

Religion and politics. If ever there were domains where alignment seems impossible, it would be these two.

As part of my research for this book, I read the platforms for both major political parties. In the spirit of being a "uniter and not a divider" and making us "stronger together," I have compiled a harmonized version—aka a mashup—of the two platforms. Here it is:

> With this platform, we reaffirm the principles that unite us in a common purpose.
>
> We believe the United States of America is unlike any other nation on earth.
>
> We meet with the same basic belief that animated the Continental Congress when they gathered in 1774: Out of many, we are one.
>
> We affirm—as did the Declaration of Independence—that all are created equal, endowed by their Creator with inalienable rights of life, liberty, and the pursuit of happiness.
>
> We believe in the Constitution as our founding document.
>
> We believe political freedom and economic freedom are indivisible. We know that diversity is not our problem—it is our promise. We respect differences of perspective, and pledge to work together to move this country forward, even when we disagree.

We believe that people are the ultimate resource—and that the people, not the government, are the best stewards of our country's God-given natural resources.

We will make America safe. We seek friendship with all peoples and all nations, but we recognize and are prepared to deal with evil in the world. We believe we are stronger and safer when America brings the world together and leads with principle and purpose.

The men and women of our military remain the world's best. We believe our military should be the best-trained, best-equipped fighting force in the world, and that we must do everything we can to honor and support our veterans.

We believe in the power of development and diplomacy. We know that only the United States can mobilize common action on a truly global scale, to take on the challenges that transcend borders, from international terrorism to climate change to health pandemics.

We are proud of our heritage as a nation of immigrants. We know that today's immigrants are tomorrow's teachers, doctors, lawyers, government leaders, soldiers, entrepreneurs, activists, PTA members, and pillars of our communities.

Based on these principles, this platform is an invitation and a roadmap. It invites every American to join us and shows the path to a stronger, safer, and more prosperous America.

This platform is optimistic because the American people are optimistic. We do not merely seek common ground—we strive to reach higher ground.

So, can you tell which sentence came from which platform?

ONE SONG – "KUMBAYA"

If the alignment cynics, skeptics, and contrarians had a theme song, it would be this One.

"What, are we going to all join hands and sing 'Kumbaya'?"

"Kumbaya" is a simple song with a humble message.

The first known recordings were in the 1920s and are archived in the Library of Congress' American Folklife Center. For several decades, it was just a children's campfire song. In the 1950s, it was recorded by dozens of artists, including Joan Baez, the Weavers, Odetta, Pete Seeger, Sweet Honey in the Rock, and many others.

In 1985, Tom Hanks and John Candy starred in a comedy movie called *Volunteers*. The movie was a satire of the idealism of the 1960s and the commingling interests of the Peace Corps and the CIA.

On August 16, 1985, Rita Kempley wrote a review of the movie in The Washington Post:

> "Tom Hanks and John Candy make war on the Peace Corps in Volunteers, a belated lampoon of '60s altruism and the idealistic young *Kumbayahoos* who went off to save the Third World."

And just like that, the word Kumbaya became shorthand for a sarcastic, cynical, and jaded view of alignment. The term caught on and has been used satirically by the likes of President Barack Obama, U.S. Ambassador John Bolton, Goldman Sachs CEO Lloyd Blankfein, and thousands more.

I certainly understand why so many people have a cynical view of alignment. Thousands of companies and other organizations probably deserve the criticism. I'm just sad that such a beautiful song came to symbolize it.

Just in case you do indeed want to "join hands and sing 'Kumbaya'" at your next meeting, here are the lyrics:

> Kumbaya, my Lord. Kumbaya.
> Kumbaya, my Lord. Kumbaya.
> Kumbaya, my Lord. Kumbaya.
> Oh, Lord, kumbaya.
> Someone's singing Lord. Kumbaya.
>
> (REPEAT TWICE)
>
> Oh, Lord, kumbaya.
> Someone's laughing, Lord. Kumbaya.
>
> (REPEAT TWICE)
>
> Oh, Lord, kumbaya.
> Someone's crying, Lord. Kumbaya.
>
> (REPEAT TWICE)
>
> Oh, Lord, kumbaya.
> Someone's praying, Lord. Kumbaya.
>
> (REPEAT TWICE)
>
> Oh, Lord, kumbaya.
> Someone's sleeping, Lord. Kumbaya.
>
> (REPEAT TWICE)
>
> Oh, Lord, kumbaya.
> Oh, Lord, kumbaya.

SØURCES

You can find a complete list of references and sources here:
https://www.shiftpoints.com/drive-one-direction-references

SHIFTPOINTS®

ABOUT SHIFTPOINTS

SHIFTPOINTS® helps companies unleash the accelerating power of alignment.

Because alignment is the ultimate competitive advantage.

Our approach is a unique mix of strategy consulting, organizational development, and executive coaching. We call it Strategy Coaching™.

In addition, we have a highly developed methodology called **Drive One Direction®** which guides clients through the process of transforming their companies.

Finally, we are intensely focused on growth. That is how we ultimately measure success.

In fact, our best client has quintupled in size. Several have doubled. Two have won "Best Place to Work" awards. One is in the Inc. 5000 Hall of Fame.

To learn more, contact us at start@shiftpoints.com.

ABOUT DAVE RAMOS

Dave Ramos is an author, speaker, and CEO of
SHIFTPOINTS, Inc.

*He is good at lots of things but is great at helping
companies unleash the accelerating power of alignment.*

Prior to founding SHIFTPOINTS, Dave applied his passion
for alignment in a broad range of settings, including large
global corporations, venture-backed start-ups, and
innovative nonprofits.

Dave started his career at IBM, where he won the
company's highest award, The Golden Circle, for excellence
in sales.

After business school, Dave joined Nortel Networks, where
he rose to be the Vice President of Global Marketing. At
Nortel, Dave won the company's highest award, The
Chairman's Award, for innovations in marketing.

He was employee #13 at AnswerLogic, a venture-backed
software company, where he led sales, marketing, and
business development.

After AnswerLogic, Dave spent four years doing pro-bono
consulting, volunteer work, and teaching.

One of his consulting clients, McLean Bible Church (a
15,000-person megachurch) asked him to join the staff full-
time. Surprising everyone, Dave accepted the job. He spent
three years as the Director of Adult Ministries and led the
church through a strategic alignment initiative.

He left the MBC staff to start The Dashboard Group, which changed its name to SHIFTPOINTS in January 2013.

Dave has an MBA from the Harvard Business School, and a BS in accounting from Drexel University.

Dave is a sought-after speaker and engages audiences with his humorous yet challenging style.

Dave is good at a lot of things but is working to become differentiatingly great at his One Thing. Contact Dave via email at start@shiftpoints.com.

DAVE RAMOS

DECIDE
ONE
THING

HOW TO DEVELOP A
DIFFERENTIATING COMPETITIVE ADVANTAGE